THE ECOLOGY OF INCLL
EDUCATION

Educators today face two major challenges. The first, is to develop an education system which meets the needs of an ever more diverse student population. The second, is to successfully implement such a system. This requires nothing less than a revolutionary transformation of current approaches taken to education.

Drawing on research-based evidence and offering over 70 concrete strategies to help educators respond to these challenges, this unique book provides a blueprint for an education system which will recognize the rights of *all* students, while engendering social cohesion and an equitable society. Broadening the scope of inclusive education, the author presents an ecological model – a system which places children at its centre and acknowledges the impacts of school, community, bureaucracy and society, to maximize opportunities for learning, and see students achieve the same levels of attainment, regardless of their gender, socio-economic status, ethnicity, religious beliefs or disability.

A timely book which addresses the concerns of teachers and educators around the globe, *The Ecology of Inclusive Education* will give its readers the knowledge and confidence they require to meet the needs of each and every learner.

David Mitchell is an Adjunct Professor at the University of Canterbury in Christchurch, New Zealand. He is the author of *What Really Works in Special and Inclusive Education* and *Diversities in Education*.

THE ECOLOGY OF INCLUSIVE EDUCATION

Strategies to Tackle the Crisis in Educating Diverse Learners

David Mitchell

Routledge
Taylor & Francis Group

LONDON AND NEW YORK

First published 2018
by Routledge
2 Park Square, Milton Park, Abingdon, Oxon OX14 4RN

and by Routledge
711 Third Avenue, New York, NY 10017

Routledge is an imprint of the Taylor & Francis Group, an informa business

© 2018 David Mitchell

British Library Cataloguing in Publication Data
A catalogue record for this book is available from the British Library

Library of Congress Cataloging in Publication Data
A catalog record for this book has been requested

ISBN: 978-1-138-08747-7 (hbk)
ISBN: 978-1-138-08748-4 (pbk)
ISBN: 978-1-315-11044-8 (ebk)

Typeset in Bembo
by Book Now Ltd, London

For my wife, Jill Mitchell, with my love and gratitude.

CONTENTS

3   Bureaucracy: 'government proposes,
bureaucracy disposes'   26

4   Communities: making connections   37

5   Schools: learning organizations with
permeable borders   40

1

INTRODUCTION: WHAT CRISIS?

Crisis! What crisis? In April 2017, I published an open letter to Ministers of Education in which I asserted that, around the globe, too many of our children are not succeeding in our schools. I went on to emphasize that this is an urgent issue that requires a radical re-thinking not only of education, but also of social policies. I believe that such changes require nothing less than a revolutionary transformation of education; piecemeal tinkering with parts of it will no longer suffice. Addressing the causes of poor outcomes and implementing remedies is very important, not only for the well-being of vulnerable children, but also for the development of an equitable society and, ultimately, to avoid the disintegration of society. I hope this book will help educators to bring their systems back from the brink of failing our most vulnerable children by maximizing opportunities for them to learn and by removing barriers.

But first, some introductory comments on the challenges educators face.

The 'big five' of diversity

So what are our challenges? Let me briefly focus on five major ones: gender, socio-economic status, ethnic minorities, religion and beliefs, and disability.

Gender. Although the achievement of boys and girls overlaps to a significant degree, in many countries boys trail behind girls. Also, there is widespread concern that girls do not tend to undertake STEM studies. At the most extreme, some countries limit, or even deny, educational opportunities for girls.

Socio-economic status. There is considerable evidence that low socio-economic status (SES) backgrounds have negative effects on children's cognitive development, social behaviours and educational achievement. Research across the world consistently concludes that SES is the strongest predictor of educational achievement.

Ethnic minorities. Most, but not all, ethnic minorities in many countries fare poorly on a wide range of educational, economic, social and health indicators. In some situations, too, they are exposed to discrimination, even persecution.

Religion and beliefs. While religion or beliefs seem to have no impact on school achievement, in some countries they can lead to discrimination and tensions.

Disability. Although there is surprisingly little information on the achievement of children with disabilities, data are increasingly being disaggregated to enable some conclusions to be drawn. Thus far, these have not been encouraging and point to the need to improve outcomes for such children.

Note, too, that in many cases it is the combination of two or more of these markers of identity that are related to discrimination or low achievement. For example, in the UK the lowest achieving groups are low SES black Caribbean boys, low SES white British boys and low SES white British girls (Strand, 2014).

We are living in an era of increasing diversity

At least in western countries, populations are becoming increasingly diverse. This trend reflects a range of factors, including the impact of globalization with its attendant mobility of labour; an upsurge of refugees fleeing conflicts or the consequences of global warming, or desertification, or seeking better economic futures; changes in peoples' belief systems; changes in demographic profiles resulting from such factors as differential fertility rates among various groups; and independent choices of identity exercised by free citizens.

Encouraging diversity vs establishing social cohesion

Striking a balance between recognizing the rights of diverse peoples and the need to maintain social cohesion constitutes a major challenge to all societies. Inevitably, this challenge falls to a significant extent upon educators. When does tolerating or encouraging diversity threaten the fabric of a cohesive society? Conversely, does the aspiration for social cohesion lead to marginalizing those who are different? To what extent should educators seek to achieve homogeneity of values, achievement and behaviour among students? To what extent should they attempt to assimilate those who are perceived to differ from the mainstream of society? What differences should they celebrate and enhance? Which ones should they seek to reduce, even eliminate?

I recognize that the answers to these questions very much depend on the contexts of particular countries. They are, nevertheless, important questions to consider.

There are economic and social benefits of improving the performances of diverse learners

In their influential book *The Spirit Level*, Richard Wilkinson and Kate Pickett made it clear that the greater the inequality in a nation, the greater the number and degree of social problems encountered, including poor educational achievement. They showed that problems that tend to be more common lower down the social ladder – such as violence, drug abuse and infant mortality – are worst in more unequal societies. Wilkinson and Pickett explained this by arguing that inequalities erode the cohesion of a society, the degree to which individual citizens are involved in their society, the strength of the social networks within it and the degree of trust and empathy between citizens. Further, as individuals internalize inequality, their psyches becoming profoundly affected by it, and that in turn affects their physical as well as their mental health, leading to attitudes and behaviours that appear as a variety of social and health problems. When these problems become widespread and those affected see no hope for the future, there is a risk of undermining the authority of the state.

In a similar vein, Barbara Ischinger (2012), Director for Education at the OECD (Organisation for Economic Co-operation and Development), has described how school failure penalizes a child for life:

> This can be seen in lower initial and lifetime earnings, more difficulties in adapting to rapidly changing knowledge-based economies, and higher risks of unemployment. The same child is also less likely to take up further learning opportunities and less able to participate fully in the civic and democratic aspects of modern societies.
>
> *(p. 15)*

And, further, there are social costs of children failing in school:

> School failure damages social cohesion and mobility, and imposes additional costs on public budgets to deal with the consequences – higher spending on public health and social support and greater criminality, among others.
>
> *(p. 15)*

Thus, as well as moral imperatives, there are substantial economic and social reasons for equalizing educational opportunities for those who are disadvantaged.

The impact of disruptive technologies

Compounding the above problems, educators should take account of the impact of disruptive technologies on the job market. Advances in computerization and other technologies mean that, at best, some jobs are likely to continue to be available but undergo significant transformations, whereas others will disappear altogether. On the plus side, technological change is likely to bring direct and indirect job creation as machines require building and maintenance, thus more wealth is created and new markets are opened.

Educators have a responsibility to prepare their students for a future where technology and its applications are likely to become increasingly sophisticated in all spheres of life. The OECD (2016) has pointed out that the impact of technological change on employment and jobs is biased towards certain types of skills. It noted that routine tasks that are easily programmable together with non-person-to-person interactions are most affected. Conversely, person-to-person services and occupations relying more on creativity, context adaptability, task discretion, social skills, and tacit cognitive capacities have been less affected.

Policies should be predicated on inclusion

Around the world, there are many instances of children being segregated on the grounds of their gender, religion, ethnicity, socio-economic status, as well as their ability. At its most extreme, some groups of children are totally or partially excluded from education, as is the case of girls in some societies or disabled children in many developing countries. Sometimes, segregation occurs as a matter of policy, for example through allowing parents to choose their children's place of schooling or through governments deciding that special schools are legitimate places to educate children with disabilities. At other times, it is (presumably) an unintended consequence of other policies, for example housing policies that lead to stratification of communities on the grounds of income. Whatever the circumstance, segregation occurs despite evidence that it at best bestows no advantages and, at worst, does harm to children.

Fortunately, around the world there are many examples of programmes that successfully accommodate student diversity. I review many of them in my two most recent books (Mitchell 2014, 2017). The challenge is twofold – how to bring these programmes to scale and how to dispense with those that are failing. This will require enlightened leadership.

Structure of this book

> To develop a complete mind: Study the art of science; study the science of art. Learn how to see. Realize that everything connects to everything else.
>
> *Leonardo DaVinci*

The 78 strategies I have selected are organized around what I term an ecological model in which everything connects to everything else, as DaVinci put it. Elsewhere, I have presented this model in the form of a spiral system to portray the relationships among the various elements that impinge on children (Figure 1). In part, it is based on Urie Bronfenbrenner's (1979) 'ecological systems theory'. Here are the main principles underlying my model:

- Individual children are at the heart of the system. They are embedded in families, which, in turn, interact with a series of other systems – classrooms, schools, communities and the broader society.
- Family factors include the interaction patterns, language, cultural capital and perceptions of the value of education held by families.
- Classroom factors include the curriculum, assessment, pedagogy, peer group influences and classroom climate.
- School factors include policies, leadership, school culture and the deployment of human and capital resources.
- Community factors include demographic features, economic resources and cultural values.
- Bureaucracy factors cover strategies within the purview of ministries or departments with responsibilities bearing on education.
- Societal factors include educational policies, resourcing and accountability mechanisms – usually the responsibility of governments.

Such systems should be 'joined up', which involves both horizontal and vertical integration. Horizontal integration requires linking systems at the same level to ensure consistency and compatibility of approach (e.g. among teachers in a school). Vertical integration requires linking more immediate, or proximal, systems with the more distal systems in which they are embedded (e.g. schools, communities and the wider society).

Influences between systems are bi-directional. Just as families influence children, so too do children influence their families, schools influence families, families influence schools, and so on. Also, it must be noted that influences at 'upper' levels in the system filter downwards through the exercise of power.

Hard-wired and optional strategies

This book contains 78 strategies, most of which should be 'hardwired', while others are optional. Examples of optional strategies include most of those listed under the classroom,

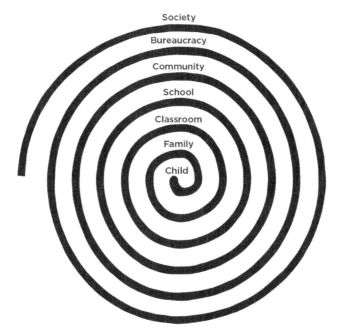

Society
Bureaucracy
Community
School
Classroom
Family
Child

FIGURE 1 An ecological model

where teachers could be expected to select strategies that suit the needs of particular children at particular times.

Conclusion

Educators have no greater responsibility than to take urgent steps to improve the quality of education received by children who are, for one reason or another, disadvantaged by circumstances over which they have no control. This is a daunting challenge to all leaders in education – in every country. It cannot be met by a business-as-usual approach nor by tinkering with some elements of an education system. Rather, it requires a radical re-thinking of all aspects of education – in schools and beyond the school gates. We know enough about the causes of low achievement and about possible remedies to take effective action.

In this book, I present strategies drawn from research and authoritative reviews that I am confident would greatly improve the opportunities to learn for our most vulnerable children, if implemented. Failure to do so risks further alienating a substantial proportion of our populations, placing them at risk of unemployment, mental health problems, criminality and even, in some cases, terrorism. We can and must resolve this crisis.

Sources

In this book, I will be condensing strategies presented in my two most recent books (Mitchell, 2014, 2017), supplementing them with a range of other material.

Sources

Bronfenbrenner, U. (1979). *The ecology of human development: Experiments by nature and design.* Cambridge, MA: Harvard University Press.

Ischinger, B. (2012). 'Foreword'. In OECD, *Equity and quality in education: Supporting disadvantaged students and schools.* Paris: OECD.

Mitchell, D. (2017). *Diversities in education.* London: Routledge.

Mitchell, D. (2014). *What really works in special and inclusive education. Second edition.* London: Routledge.

OECD (2016). *Future of work in figures.* Paris. URL: www.oecd.org/employment/ministerial/future-of-work-in-figures.htm

Strand, S. (2014). 'Ethnicity, gender, social class and achievement gaps at age 16: Intersectionality and "getting it" for the white working class.' *Research Papers in Education, 29*(2), 131–171.

Wilkinson, R.G., & Pickett, K. (2009). *The spirit level: Why more equal societies almost always do better.* London: Allen Lane.

2

SOCIETY

Unity in diversity

Although Margaret Thatcher once infamously stated that there is no such thing as society, I am more inclined to accept the *Oxford Dictionary*'s perspective that societies do exist and may be defined as 'The aggregate of people living together in a more or less ordered community.' Wikipedia extends this definition as follows:

> A society is a group of people involved in persistent social interaction, or a large social group sharing the same geographical or social territory, typically subject to the same political authority and dominant cultural expectations. Societies are characterized by patterns of relationships ... between individuals who share a distinctive culture and institutions; a given society may be described as the sum total of such relationships among its constituent of members.

The American philosopher and sociologist George Herbert Mead added another perspective very pertinent to the themes I address in this book. In his words, 'We are indefinitely different from each other, but our differences make interaction possible. Society is unity in diversity.'

Consideration of societal influences on the education of diverse learners turns our attention to the nature and location of authority and power. Across the world, there is a bewildering array of instruments exerting power in the governing of societies. Models range from democracies (of various stripes), through theocracies and plutocracies, to absolute monarchies and dictatorships. In turn, countries vary in the extent to which power is retained at the centre or shared or devolved to the local level, often through federal systems. This balance between centralization and devolution is often in a state of flux and can lead to tensions.

Whichever political model is followed, power is usually exercised through legislation and related policy determinations. To a greater or lesser extent, these instruments are influenced by international Conventions, usually emerging from the United Nations and its various bodies (see **Strategy 1**). They also reflect societies' dominant cultures and their commitments to human rights and distributive justice. In turn, historical and economic factors are also in play in determining these commitments. As well, the vagaries of different electoral systems and their vulnerability to lobbying and media (including social media) determine the extent to which governments reflect the will of the people and are prepared and able to implement the 18 strategies outlined in this chapter.

Sources

Diversities in Education, Chapter 1. In *George Herbert Mead: Selected writings*. University of Chicago Press, 1964.

Strategy 1: Recognize the rights and freedoms specified in relevant international Conventions generated by the Universal Declaration of Human Rights

Rationale

Consideration of society's responsibilities towards children who are disadvantaged must be predicated on human rights. These inform us as to what we may, must, and must not do to others and what we may expect of others in their behaviour towards us. In 1948, the United Nations agreed to the *Universal Declaration of Human Rights* (UDHR). Article 7 is of particular relevance to the theme of this book. It reads:

> All are equal before the law and are entitled without any discrimination to equal protection of the law. All are entitled to equal protection against any discrimination in violation of this Declaration and against any incitement to such discrimination.

Since 1948, the commitment articulated in the UDHR has been translated into law – whether in the form of treaties, customary international law, general principles, regional agreements and domestic law – through which human rights are expressed and guaranteed. It has formed the basis of a wide range of *Conventions* or other instruments summarized below.

The strategy

Governments should accept their obligations under international instruments, including the following:

- The 1960 *Convention against Discrimination in Education*, which includes the obligation 'To ensure, by legislation where necessary, that there is no discrimination in the admission of pupils to educational institutions' and 'To ensure that the standards of education are equivalent in all public educational institutions of the same level, and that the conditions relating to the quality of the education provided are also equivalent.'
- The 1965 *International Convention on the Elimination of All Forms of Racial Discrimination*.
- The 1981 *Declaration on the Elimination of All Forms of Intolerance and of Discrimination Based on Religion or Belief*.
- The 1989 *Convention on the Rights of the Child*, which requires education be directed to: 'The development of the child's personality, talents and mental and physical abilities to their fullest potential'.
- The 1990 *International Convention on the Protection of the Rights of All Migrant Workers and Members of Their Families*.
- The 1999 *International Covenant on Economic, Social and Cultural Rights*, which states that 'Education is both a human right in itself and an indispensable means of realizing other human rights'.
- UNESCO's 2001 *Universal Declaration on Cultural Diversity*.
- The 2008 *Convention on the Rights of People with Disabilities*, which emphasizes inclusive education.

Source

Diversities in education, Chapter 1. Op cit.

Strategy 2: Ensure that reason and evidence determine educational policies and practices

Rationale

As I have pointed out in my recent books and as John Hattie (2009) has emphasized, educators are increasingly expected to draw upon credible data and research-based evidence in planning, implementing and evaluating their teaching. In Europe, for example, since 2010 there has been a project, Evidence-informed Policy and Practice in Education in Europe, with 34 partner organizations from 24 countries, together with four affiliates from outside Europe. This project aims to broker knowledge using common reference tools and approaches, as well as exchanging good practices, data and evidence from relevant European agencies and national-level resources. In the United States, the 2015 Every Student Succeeds Act (ESSA), defined four categories of evidence based on their relative strength. Further, the recent establishment of centres specializing in gathering and disseminating evidence-based education policies and practices provides further support for the growing commitment to evidence-based education in the United States.

As well as empirical, research-based evidence, I recognize that educationists should also be basing their policies and practices on reasoning derived from philosophical and theoretical analyses.

The strategy

Throughout education systems, evidence-based approaches to improving the performance of learners who are underachieving and/or manifesting significant behavioural problems should be adopted. I therefore recommend:

1 Establishing national and/or regional Clearing Houses, with four main responsibilities: (a) developing a repository of evidence-informed strategies in the field of education; (b) responding to requests from participating schools and disseminating the implementation and results of strategies that are put in place; (c) periodically compiling syntheses of strategies relevant to the national or regional situations; and (d) recommending research on extending evidence on effective educational strategies.
2 Inviting participating schools to appoint Research Coordinators whose responsibilities would include: (a) setting up committees to identify specific challenges arising from identified under-achievement and behavioural problems within their schools; (b) seeking advice and guidance on possible evidence-informed strategies from the Central Clearing house; (c) implementing selected strategies and evaluating their impact; and (d) reporting on the implementation and impact of these strategies to the central Clearing House.

This proposal has some similarities to the UK's Coalition for Evidence-based Education. This is an alliance of researchers, policy makers and practitioners interested in improving the way research evidence is accessed, and used, across the sector (see www.cebenetwork.org/).

Sources

What really works, Chapter 1. Op cit.
Diversities in education, Chapter 1. Op cit.
Hattie, J. (2009). *Visible learning*. Routledge.

Strategy 3: Develop wraparound services

Rationale

In the past two decades or so, there has been a distinct trend towards 'joined-up thinking' in providing human services. 'Wraparound' was originally developed in the United States in the 1980s as a means of maintaining youth with serious emotional and behavioural disorders in their homes and communities. It has since spread widely to many countries.

Wraparound is a system-level intervention that quite literally aims to 'wrap' services around children and their families to address their problems in an ecologically comprehensive and coordinated way. In developing joined-up services for disadvantaged children and young persons it is essential to see them as being embedded in various systems: their families, classrooms, schools and communities, indeed the theme of this book. It is manifested in the move from fragmentation to integrated intervention and from narrowly-focused and special-oriented, 'silo' services to comprehensive approaches.

The strategy

The main features of the wraparound approach are as follows:

- employment of a structured and individualized team planning process;
- development of plans designed to meet the identified needs of young people and their caregivers and siblings;
- emphasis on team-based planning aimed at developing problem-solving skills, coping skills and self-efficacy of the young people and their families;
- utilization of skilled facilitators to guide teams through a defined planning process;
- integration of young people into their communities and building their families' natural social support networks;
- employment of culturally appropriate practices;
- recognition of the strengths of young people and their families;
- employment of evidence-based treatments within the process;
- monitoring of progress on measurable indicators of success and changing the plan as necessary;
- access to flexible funding; and
- focusing on, and being accountable for, outcomes.

Implementing and sustaining wraparound is both complex and difficult. It requires dealing with such challenges as: (a) re-negotiating relationships among providers, consumers (i.e. families) and the community; (b) developing a single, comprehensive plan that defines how each agency involved will work with the child and family; (c) obtaining and allocating funding among several agencies; (d) satisfying the mandates of agencies with different missions; (e) managing different, perhaps conflicting, priorities between families and agency-based professionals; and (f) providing appropriate training of the professionals involved.

Governments should develop legislation and policies to mandate the wraparound approach, while ministries or departments should ensure its implementation.

Sources

National Wraparound Implementation Center. URL: /www.nwic.org/
What really works, Chapter 26. Op cit.

Strategy 4: Develop equitable funding models

Rationale

As I noted in Chapter 1, there are economic benefits in improving the performances of diverse learners. It therefore makes sense to invest in strategies likely to redress disadvantages among such learners. Since the 1990s, an increasing number of countries has introduced weighted funding formulae that take into consideration the importance of ensuring equity and quality across their education systems. This involves consideration of several factors, including (a) which children should receive the most direct or indirect assistance; (b) how disadvantage is determined, and at what level(s) in the education system; (c) how the quantum of funding is determined; (d) how often special funding is reviewed; and (e) the strings attached to it.

The strategy

School funding formulae may be assessed in relation to six criteria.

1   *Transparency* refers to the situation when stakeholders have easily available information on the amount of funding each administrative unit receives, the basis for this allocation and how these resources are used.
2   *Adequacy* refers to resources being sufficient to achieve a specified standard of education for specified categories of students. New models that link educational revenues, resources and outcomes need to be developed. In other words, there is a need for rigorous cost–benefit analyses.
3   *Efficiency* means achieving the highest feasible output from a given volume of resources. This requires selecting the least-cost combination of inputs for producing a given amount of educational output.
4   *Equity* refers to the fairness with which resources in education are allocated and used. *Horizontal equity* is the equal resourcing of pupils with similar characteristics or learning needs, while *vertical equity* refers to differentially funding students according to differences in their needs.
5   *Robustness* means that an allocation mechanism should not be open to distortions, in particular the possibility of 'gaming the system' by the deliberate falsification of information or by the employment of unreliable means of gathering data. Moral hazard is another source of distortion to be avoided. This may occur when there is information asymmetry, i.e. where the risk-taking party to a transaction knows more about its intentions than the party paying the consequences of the risk.
6   *Freedom from unintended consequences* refers to funding mechanisms that lead to erroneous or distorted messages regarding the quality of education in particular schools. However, it is difficult to envisage any system of differential funding not being subject to such unintended consequences, even when they are based on erroneous assumptions.

Source

Diversities in education, Chapters 3 and 6. Op cit.

Strategy 5: Manage school choice to avoid segregation

Rationale

There are basically two options when deciding which schools children should attend: (1) the school nearest the family residence, or (2) any school chosen by the child's parents/caregivers. Respectively, these are referred to as school zoning and school choice. In making policy decisions regarding school attendance, governments should take account of how this might impact on students' achievement. There is considerable evidence that achievement is lower in schools where most students come from similar low-SES or ethnic minority backgrounds, compared with the same students' achievement were they to receive their education in more mixed school environments.

On the one hand, if a school zoning policy is followed, this often means that schools are stratified according to SES and ethnicity. On the other hand, providing full parental school choice can result in segregating students by ability or SES background (OECD, 2012). For example, there is some evidence that giving parents a choice over schools actually increases the social divide. This was demonstrated in an English study which found that the majority of poor parents picked schools that were close to their home, whereas nearly half of middle-class parents opted for schools based on academic record (Burgess et al., 2015).

The strategy

It is important that any policies on which schools children should attend are designed and managed to achieve a balance between choice and equity.

The OECD has argued that there are different options possible, including (a) controlled choice schemes that combine parental choice and ensure a more diverse distribution of students, (b) incentives to make disadvantaged students attractive to high-quality schools, (c) school selection mechanisms, (d) vouchers and (e) tax credits. Policies are also required to improve disadvantaged families' access to information about schools and to support them in making informed choices. Policy makers should note there is clear evidence that reducing school segregation does not reduce the performance of high achieving students.

Nijmegen, in the Netherlands, provides an example of controlled choice. Here, a central subscription system is used to assign students to primary schools, with the aim of reaching 30% of disadvantaged students in each school.

Sources

Burgess, S., Greaves, E., Vignoles, A., & Wilson, D. (2015). 'What parents want: School preferences and school choice.' *Economic Journal, 125*(587), 1262–1289.
Diversities in education, Chapters 3 and 4. Op cit.
OECD (2012). *Equity and quality in education: Supporting disadvantaged students and schools.* Paris.

Strategy 6: Give priority to quality early childhood education
Rationale

There is abundant evidence as to the effectiveness of *quality* early childhood education. For example, in England, Sylva et al. (2004) found that the benefits of pre-school education largely persisted through to age 11. Attendance at pre-school was beneficial for both academic and social/behavioural outcomes, as well as children's' self-perceptions. The benefits were greater for boys, pupils with special educational needs and pupils from disadvantaged backgrounds. However, for some of the outcomes, notably English, Mathematics and 'Hyperactivity', only pre-schools of medium or high quality afforded lasting effects. Similarly, Melhuish et al. (2017) found that early childhood education was associated with benefits for several aspects of socio-emotional development, with children who attended pre-schools showing fewer emotional symptoms, more pro-social behaviour and fewer peer problems. This was particularly true of children from disadvantaged homes. In addition, there were substantial effects upon child development outcomes associated with parents providing rich home learning environments, and these effects were often similar in size to the effects of early childhood education (see also **Strategy 77**).

The strategy

It is essential that early childhood education meets quality standards. New Zealand provides examples of such standards (Education Review Office, 2016) and these are listed below:

- A clear vision sets direction for the service.
- The philosophy, vision and associated goals and plans are influenced by the aspirations parents and families have for their children.
- Self-reviews are ongoing, responsive to identified priorities, include all aspects of the operation of the service over time, and focus on the effectiveness of processes and practices.
- The service's priorities and goals are strongly linked to positive learning outcomes for children.
- The service has up-to-date policies and procedures that support the recruitment, management and professional learning and development of competent managers and teachers.
- The service has effective systems to monitor physical and emotional health and safety for all involved in the service.
- Management promotes equity and social justice for children and their families through cross-cultural development and understanding.

Sources

Diversities in education, Chapter 1. Op cit.

Education Review Office (2016). *Quality in early childhood services.* Wellington, New Zealand.

Melhuish, E., Gardiner, J., & Morris, S. (2017). *Study of Early Education and Development (SEED): Impact study on early education use and child outcomes up to age three.* Research report. Oxford: NatCen Social Research and University of Oxford.

Sylva, K., Melhuish, E.C., Sammons, P., Siraj-Blatchford, I., & Taggart, B. (2004). *The Effective Provision of Pre-school Education (EPPE) Project: Final report.* London: DfES/Institute of Education, University of London.

Strategy 7: Develop early intervention programmes for infants and toddlers

Rationale

In **Strategy 6**, I outlined the importance of early childhood education for *all* children. I now turn to targeted early intervention for infants and toddlers with disabilities and delays. These programmes are gaining increasing recognition as part of the range of human services to which families should have access. They may be defined as 'systematic strategies aimed at promoting the optimal development of infants and toddlers with special needs and at enhancing the functioning of their families or caregivers' (Mitchell & Brown, p. xii).

Evidence from the United States is supportive of these programmes, although there are some mixed results. For example, in a randomized control trial, the Abecedarian Project employed a comprehensive education, healthcare and family support programme to focus on low-income, multi-risk families. It resulted in a reduced incidence of delayed cognitive development, with the most vulnerable children benefitting the most. The long-standing Head Start programme has also reported positive results in reading and mathematics for its participants, compared with peers in the same SES group, although they still lagged behind those children from high SES homes. However, these results need to be analyzed in more depth, for there is evidence that some of the gains made fade over time and some writers argue that we need to know much more about how early intervention actually works, in particular, the connections between its components and particular child outcomes. This is very important when it comes to policy decisions on how programmes should be scaled up to be cost-effective.

The strategy

There is no one model of early intervention. Programmes are quite diverse in terms of which agencies control them, their clientele, their mode of service delivery, assessment methods, curriculum design, cultural sensitivity, staff qualifications and training, and relationships with parents/caregivers. The model I favour is one that emphasizes:

- learning opportunities that enhance children's development;
- parent-mediated child learning opportunities that strengthen child and parent competence and confidence; and
- early intervention practitioner use of family-centred capacity-building practices (Dunst & Espe-Sherwindt, 2017).

Sources

Diversities in education, Chapter 3. Op cit.

Dunst, C.J., & Espe-Sherwindt, M. (2017). 'Contemporary early intervention models, research, and practice for infants and toddlers with disabilities and delays' In J.M. Kauffman, D.P. Hallahan, & P.C. Pullen (eds), *Handbook of special education*, Second edition (pp. 831–849). Routledge.

Mitchell, D., & Brown, R.I. (eds) (1991). *Early intervention studies for young children with special needs*. Chapman & Hall.

Strategy 8: Take steps to increase SES by reducing poverty, increasing employment and improving the education levels of the populace

Rationale

Socio-economic status (SES) refers to an individual's or family's economic and social position in relation to others. It is based on three factors: income, education and occupation. Thus, poverty forms a subset of SES and is usually, but not always, highly correlated with it. While I recognize that to improve the life-chances of children from low-SES families all three factors must be addressed, this strategy focuses on poverty.

The deleterious effects of poverty on child development have been well established in research, with it being identified as being among the most powerful risk factors for development. Children exposed to poverty have poorer cognitive outcomes and are at higher risk for antisocial behaviours and mental disorders. It has a negative impact on brain development: it has been shown to be associated with smaller white and cortical gray matter and hippocampal and amygdala volumes. In addition, poverty is strongly associated with a number of risk factors implicated in poor developmental outcomes, such as unsupportive parenting, poor nutrition and education, lack of caregiver education and high levels of traumatic and stressful life events. These findings accentuate the importance of providing children from low-SES backgrounds with appropriate stimulation and acceptable levels of stress, particularly in their early development when they are most vulnerable to adverse environmental conditions.

The strategy

Governments possess a range of instruments for reducing poverty.

- At the broadest level, they can enact policies to expand growth in their economies, relying on the indirect effect of putting more money into the pockets of the poorer members of society, or maybe by putting more money in the pockets of the richer members of society who, in turn, would be expected to invest in plant, equipment and labour.
- Other financial instruments are also available: adjusting taxation rates, adjusting welfare benefits, increasing housing subsidies, financing paid parental leave and child support, increasing minimum wages and reducing the costs of childcare and healthcare.
- Provide adequate funds to the education system to facilitate its work with low-SES students and their families (see **Strategy 4**). (It has been estimated that a one-year increase in the average educational attainment of a country's population would increase annual per capita GDP growth by between 2% and 2.5%.
- Provide adequate vocational guidance and work placement opportunities in secondary schools (see **Strategy 18**).

Source

Diversities in education, Chapter 3. Op cit.

Strategy 9: Introduce free and/or subsidized school meals for low-SES students

Rationale

Too many children come to school without having had breakfast or with either no or inadequate lunches. For example, recent New Zealand data showed that 25% of children from low-SES homes came to school with some degree of food need, with around 12% not eating breakfast at home every day. Moreover, they were also more likely to consume soft drinks (sodas) and fast food of limited nutritional value (Ministry of Health, 2009). Despite this, New Zealand does not offer free or subsidized school meals, although some schools have non-government programmes.

A large body of evidence shows that diet quality follows a socio-economic gradient. Whereas higher-quality diets are associated with greater affluence, persons of lower SES tend to consume energy-dense diets that are nutrient-poor. For example, whole grains, lean meats, fish, low-fat dairy products and fresh vegetables and fruit are more likely to be consumed by groups of higher SES. In contrast, the consumption of refined grains and added fats has been associated with lower SES. The provision of nutritious food to children has effects in a number of areas including attendance at school, concentration, memory, mood, mental health and test scores in various subjects. Effects are consistently largest for nutritionally at-risk or undernourished children.

School meal programmes are very common in many countries, especially in Europe (including the United Kingdom), but also in Russia, Hong Kong, Brazil and Chile. These usually comprise school lunches (often cooked), but can also include both breakfast and lunch in some countries. Programmes vary in terms of targeting (by age and or income) or universality. For example, in Sweden, Finland and Estonia, free school meals have been available for all children, irrespective of their SES. (It is arguable that such programmes avoid any stigmatization that may be associated with being singled out.) In contrast, the Free School Meal scheme in the United Kingdom is based on a family being in receipt of any means-tested benefit. Across Europe, school lunch nutrition standards are the basis for improving the nutritional intake of all school children (www.eufic.org/en/healthy-living/article/school-lunch-standards-in-europe).

Finally, growing rates of obesity in children – especially among those from low-SES homes – have encouraged governments to provide healthier, more balanced school meals.

The strategy

Quite simply, the strategy is, in the first instance, to introduce free and/or subsidized school meals for low-SES students. Then, serious consideration should be given to making them universally available.

Sources

Diversities in education, Chapter 3. Op cit.
Ministry of Health (2009). *A focus on the health of Maori and Pacific children: Key findings of the 2006/07 New Zealand Health Survey*. Wellington, New Zealand.

Strategy 10: Prevent and respond to gender-based violence

Rationale

Sadly, gender-based violence is a global phenomenon that knows no geographical, cultural, social, economic, ethnic or other boundary. According to the United Nations, it disproportionately affects girls and women and is a major obstacle to the achievement of gender equality. For example, National Violence Against Children surveys in Swaziland, Tanzania, Zimbabwe and Kenya revealed that 28–38% of girls and 9–18% of boys were subjected to unwanted sexual experiences before the age of 18, which placed them at greater risk of contracting HIV. Evidence suggests that girls are at greater risk of sexual violence, while boys are at higher risk of physical violence in schools. Data from 40 low- and middle-income countries show that up to 10% of adolescent girls aged 15–19 reported incidents of forced sexual intercourse or other sexual acts in the previous year, some initiated by teachers. In some countries, violence in, on the way to, or associated with school are important reasons why girls do not enroll or attend school.

Sexual violence in schools is not limited to low-income countries. For example, in the United Kingdom one in three 16- to 18-year-olds is reported to have experienced unwanted sexual touching in schools. According to a US survey of adults, as many as one in three girls and one in seven boys were sexually abused at some point in their childhood. Most perpetrators were acquaintances, but as many as 47% were family or extended family members.

As well as unwanted pregnancies, the experience or even the threat of school-related gender-based violence directed at girls often results in irregular attendance, dropout, truancy, poor school performance and low self-esteem, which may follow into their adult lives.

The strategy

Governments should develop policies to prevent and respond to gender-based violence. These should include establishing monitoring frameworks with standardized indicators to establish the extent of school-related gender-based violence. Although girls are more likely than boys to be victims of violence, both should be attended to.

Addressing such violence requires a multi-sectoral approach with collaboration across education, health, social welfare and youth sectors (see also **Strategy 3**).

School authorities should be vigilant in detecting, preventing and dealing with gender-based violence, both within school precincts and on students' travel to and from school.

Teachers should be aware of the common indicators or disclosures of sexual and physical abuse and report these to relevant authorities.

Source

Diversities in education, Chapter 2. Op cit.

Strategy 11: Promote the maintenance of students' first language by employing Mother Tongue-Based Multilingual Education

Rationale

Mother Tongue-Based Multilingual Education (MTB-MLE) requires the use of the mother tongue as the language of instruction in the classroom. It refers to schooling that makes use of the language or languages that children are most familiar with. This policy is based on the assumption that by starting in the language they know best, children will be able to build a strong foundation at school, which then enables them to make an effective transition into the national language in due course. It also increases the likelihood that they will enjoy school more, feel more at home, and show increased self-esteem. Furthermore, parents can help more with homework and participate in school activities.

Research shows that children learn best in their mother tongue as a prelude to and complement of bilingual and multilingual education. It also shows that children's ability to learn a second language does not suffer when their mother tongue is the primary language of instruction throughout primary school. It would seem that fluency and literacy in the mother tongue lays a cognitive and linguistic foundation for learning additional languages. There is growing evidence that bilingualism (or multilingualism) may actually confer advantages to the developing brain. Because bilingual children switch between languages, they develop the ability to effectively manage higher cognitive processes, such as problem-solving and memory.

The strategy

MTB-MLE can take many forms but, in general, the longer a child is able to learn in and through its mother tongue(s) the greater the educational benefits that can be expected. A compendium of examples produced by UNESCO (2008) attests to a growing interest in promoting MTB-MLE.

Where feasible, children whose mother-tongue is different from the country's language of instruction should be taught in their mother tongue. Equal importance is given to learning in and through both languages and children learn how to take full advantage of their multilingualism and biliteracy.

The availability of teachers fluent in the range of mother tongues presented by children will place limits on implementing this recommendation. The length of time mother-tongue instruction is employed will depend on individual children's responsiveness and parents'/ caregivers' wishes. Decisions have to be made as to the timing and amount of parallel instruction in the country's usual language of instruction.

Source

Diversities in education, Chapter 4. Op cit.
UNESCO (2008). *Mother tongue matters: Local language as a key to effective learning*. Paris.

Strategy 12: In multilingual countries, consider teaching two and possibly three languages

Rationale

In terms of 'official languages', several countries stand out. These include Luxembourg where most people speak Luxemburgish and French and German are co-official languages, while English is compulsory for students to learn at school. Singapore has four official languages: English, Mandarin Chinese, Malay and Tamil; however, hardly any people actually speak all four and English is the main lingua franca. Switzerland has four official languages: German, French, Italian and Romansh. All Swiss children have to learn a second official language and English by the fifth year of primary school.

Clearly, in terms of multi-lingual countries such as those cited, citizens should be fluent in more than their mother tongue and preferably in most if not all the official languages. This will enable them to communicate with and better understand their compatriots, thus contributing to social cohesion. Further, in today's globalized world, *all* children benefit from a multilingual education offering them an opportunity to become fluent in their mother tongues as well as in the state's official language, and one or more foreign languages. This allows them to pursue higher education, to communicate easily in more than one language, through different media and to contribute meaningfully to society and to an increasingly globalized world (see also **Strategy 71**).

The strategy

Research into teaching and learning three languages is quite complex and provides suggestions as to strategies to pursue. According to Dyssegaard et al. (2015):

- The learning process of acquiring a second language (L2) differs greatly from that of third language learning. The main difference is that third language (L3) learners can use two languages as base languages in third language acquisition while second language (L2) learners can only use their first language as the base language.
- Students in immersion programmes who are learning an L2 and an L3 at an early age develop age appropriate skills in their L1 and L2 at the same time.
- When one of the languages a bilingual learner knows is a minority language, then they obtain better results in L3 when their minority language is valued and used at home.
- High levels of proficiency in L1 and L2 has a positive impact on L3 acquisition.

Sources

Diversities in education, Chapter 4. Op cit.

Dyssegaard, et al. (2015). *A systematic review of the impact of multiple language teaching, prior language experience and acquisition order on students' language proficiency in primary and secondary school*. Copenhagen: Danish Clearinghouse for Educational Research.

Strategy 13: Ensure that government-funded schools have a secular character

Rationale

The role of religion in education is a sensitive, contentious and complex issue. From the outset, I recognize that this strategy may not be acceptable to some readers, given their beliefs and the histories and the current make-up of their education systems.

In arriving at this strategy, I took seven principles into account:

1   Many countries are religiously diverse and rapidly becoming even more so. Account must also be taken of the variation in importance people place upon religion in their lives.
2   Cognizance must be taken of the rights of individuals to pursue their own religions or beliefs. This means eliminating religious intolerance, discrimination, prejudice and persecution. At the same time, it must be recognized that tensions arise between competing rights, in particular the potential conflict between the rights of parents to determine the religious education of their children and the state's obligations to ensure children receive an education in conformity with the requirements spelled out in human rights instruments.
3   The concept of indoctrination lies at the heart of deciding what role, if any, religion should play in education. The essence of indoctrination is that it allows little questioning of whatever belief is being promulgated and takes place without recourse to evidence. It has no place in education.
4   Whatever approach to religious education is adopted, it should always take account of children's cognitive maturity. They should not be required to accept beliefs before they are capable of seeking and evaluating evidence for them.
5   Religious instruction has no place in schools supported by the state.
6   In free, democratic societies, parents have the right to seek out religious instruction in their own faith for their children. I accept that parents or caregivers can make such arrangements, provided they do not occur under the aegis of the state's education system. I would hope that in raising their children in a specific religious tradition, parents take steps to ensure their child does not develop an exclusivist religious belief.
7   Educators should seek to develop 'reflective pluralism' in their students through engaging with people and groups whose religious practices are fundamentally different from their own.

The strategy

Schools that select students on the basis of their religion or include religious instruction in school hours should not be provided with government funding.

Source

Diversities in education, Chapter 5. Op cit.

Strategy 14: Ensure that all children with disabilities receive education

Rationale

Children with disabilities are among the most disadvantaged in terms of missing out on education, particularly in developing countries. This can be attributed to several factors, including education systems that are not adapted or equipped to meet their needs, the lack of accessible school buildings, untrained teachers, problems with transport, inflexible curricula and examination systems and the continuing stigma around disability. The cumulative result of these factors is the low participation rate of children with disabilities in education. For example, while India has achieved close to universal enrolment in primary education, a 2009 survey showed that out of 2.9 million children with disabilities, 990,000 (34%) were out of school.

Fortunately, many countries are beginning to address this situation, spurred along by their ratification of the UN's 2006 *Convention on the Rights of People with Disabilities*. This recognizes the right of all children with disabilities both to be included in the general education systems and to receive the individual support they require. As well, Article 24 of the Convention stresses the need for governments to ensure equal access to an 'inclusive education system at all levels' (see **Strategy 15**). Furthermore, countries are increasingly recognizing that they cannot achieve the UN's Millennium Development Goal of universal completion of primary education without ensuring access to education for children with disabilities.

The strategy

Where children with disabilities are not enrolled in education or when they have low rates of school completion, systemic and school-level changes should be initiated in order to:

- ensure equal access to quality education;
- remove physical and attitudinal barriers;
- provide reasonable accommodation and specialist support services;
- provide teachers with practical training and ongoing support;
- identify the level and nature of need, so that the correct support and accommodations can be introduced;
- make curricula, learning materials, and assessments accessible; and
- focus on educating children with disabilities as close to the mainstream as possible (see World Health Organization & World Bank, 2011).

Finally, responsibility for the education of children with disabilities should rest with Ministries/Departments of Education. This should not preclude active collaboration with other ministries/departments, such as Health and Social Welfare, in order to provide wraparound services (see **Strategy 3**).

Sources

Diversities in education, Chapter 6. Op cit.

World Health Organization & World Bank (2011). *World report on disability*. Geneva: World Health Organization.

Strategy 15: Promote inclusive education for learners with special educational needs

Rationale

At its most basic, inclusive education means educating all learners within regular education settings. However, it means much more than mere placement. Rather, it means putting in place a whole suite of provisions. With reference to learners with special education needs, the idea of inclusive education reflects three main factors. First, if it is handled appropriately, they will gain academically and socially and improve their self-esteem. Second, those who do not have special needs will gain an appreciation of the diversity of their society, a greater recognition of social justice and equality, and a more caring attitude. Third, learners with special educational needs have a right to be educated alongside their peers who do not have special needs. It is thus seen as a matter of equity and social justice.

The strategy

The following 'magic formula' summarizes what is required for inclusive education (IE):

$$IE = V + P + 5As + S + R + L.$$

Vision: IE requires a commitment on the part of educators at all levels of the system to its underlying philosophy and a willingness to implement it.

Placement: Placement in an age-appropriate classroom in the learner's neighbourhood school is necessary.

Adapted curriculum: This includes modifications, substitutions, omissions and compensations to the general curriculum.

Adapted assessment: Learners should be assessed on what they have been taught and it should be as much 'assessment for learning' as 'assessment of learning'.

Adapted teaching: IE challenges educators to develop a wide repertoire of evidence-informed teaching strategies. These are the focus of many of the classroom strategies outlined in Chapter 6.

Acceptance: IE relies on acceptance of the right of learners with special educational needs to be educated in general education classrooms and to receive equitable resourcing.

Access: For learners with physical disabilities to be included, adequate access to classrooms must be provided.

Support: IE requires support from a team of professionals, the composition of which depends on the needs of the learners. It also requires active support from parents/caregivers.

Resources: IE requires high levels of resourcing, but no more than would be available to support a learner with special educational needs in a special school.

Leadership: To bring all of the above elements together, leadership is required at all levels: government, national education departments or ministries, provincial or state departments, districts, school principals and classroom teachers.

Source

What really works, Chapter 27. Op cit.

Strategy 16: Ensure that students with special educational needs have access to the general curriculum

Rationale

With the advent of inclusive education policies and practices (**Strategy 15**), many countries are addressing the need for students with special educational needs to have access to the general education curriculum, as far as possible. For example, in the United States, all students, including those with significant cognitive disabilities, must have the opportunity to participate and progress in the general curriculum. Individual Education Plans must include academic and functional goals, designed to enable the child to make progress in the general education curriculum. Similarly, within the United Kingdom, Scotland seeks to ensure that students with special educational needs can access the common curriculum framework, while at the same time ensuring appropriate and targeted support. In contrast, some countries have separate curricula: one for mainstream students and the other for students with special educational needs. The Flemish community within Belgium is one such example.

The strategy

To make the general curriculum accessible to students with disabilities adaptations such as the following should be made to content, teaching materials and the responses expected from learners:

- accommodations are changes made to the teaching in order to provide a student with access to information without changing the instructional level or content (e.g. enlarging the print, providing oral versions of material and using calculators);
- modifications, where a student with a disability may be working on modified course content, but the subject area remains the same as for the rest of the class;
- substitutions (e.g. using Braille for written materials);
- omissions (e.g. omitting very complex work);
- additions (e.g. teaching self-care skills, mobility);
- streamlining the curriculum by reducing its size or breadth, but still emphasizing the key points;
- employing the same activity but infusing IEP objectives for students with disabilities.

Underlying these adaptations is the principle of differentiation. This is the process of varying content, activities, teaching, learning, methods and resources to take into account the range of interests, needs and experiences of individual students (National Council for Curriculum and Assessment, 2007, p. 8) (see also **Strategy 75**).

See also Universal Design for Learning (**Strategy 52**).

Sources

National Council for Curriculum and Assessment (2007). *Guidelines for teachers of students with mild general learning disabilities*: Dublin.
What really works, Chapter 27. Op cit.

Strategy 17: Ensure that students with special educational needs have access to the national or state assessments

Rationale

Just as I argued in **Strategy 16** that students with disability needs should have access to the general curriculum, it follows that they should also have access to the same assessment regime as other children – but with adaptations.

Until recently, in the United States, accountability in special education was defined in terms of progress in meeting IEP goals. This all changed with the Individuals with Disabilities Education Act of 1997, which required all students, including those with disabilities, to participate in their states' accountability systems. Subsequent legislation, however, required the provision of alternate assessment for students who could not participate in state or district assessments with or without accommodations. Districts were permitted to measure up to 3% of their students using alternate assessments (1% against alternate achievement standards and 2% against modified standards).

In England, tests set for assessment at the end of Key Stages 2 and 3 (for students aged 11 and 14, respectively) are designed to monitor attainment targets for each of the National Curriculum subjects, and are expected to be accessible to the vast majority of students, including those with disabilities. However, children in Key Stage 2 working at level 1 or below of the National Curriculum's eight-level scale are assessed by teacher assessment alone. Similarly, at Key Stage 3, students working at or below level 2 of the National Curriculum scale are assessed by teacher assessment and not by statutory national testing.

The strategy

Basically, there are two types of adjustments:

Assessments with accommodations. These involve making changes to the assessment process, but not the essential content. Some students may be awarded extra time or permitted to take supervised rest periods during the examination. Visually impaired students may have large print or braille versions of papers. Other students may have questions read to them; flashcards may be used to assist hearing-impaired candidates in mental arithmetic tests; or typewritten, word processed or transcribed responses may be accepted from students unable to write.

Alternate assessments. These are for the small number of students with disabilities unable to participate in the regular State assessment, even with appropriate accommodations. They refer to materials collected under several circumstances, including: teacher observations, samples of students' work produced during regular classroom instruction and standardized performance tasks.

Source

What really works, Chapter 27. Op cit.

Strategy 18: Develop policies on transition from school to post-school situations for children at risk of not being in education, employment and training when they leave school

Rationale

People who are Not in Employment, Education or Training (NEET) when they leave school pose a challenge to most countries. The OECD (2010) claims that 26 million 15- to 24-year-olds in OECD countries are not in employment, education or training. *The Economist* puts the total global figure at 290 million who are neither working nor studying. However, there is considerable variation in the rate of NEETs across the OECD. Figures range from 4% (Netherlands) to 30% (Turkey).

A number of characteristics are associated with a higher likelihood of being a long-term NEET. These include living in the most deprived neighbourhoods, living with a single or a non-working parent, leaving school with minimal or low qualifications and becoming a parent between the ages of 16 and 18 (Quintini, Martin, & Martin (2007).

NEET has economic, personal and social outcomes, including:

- prolonged dependence, with young people failing to establish a sense of direction;
- poor physical and mental health outcomes; and
- greater use of drugs, alcohol and higher levels of criminal activity.

The strategy

Policies should be put in place to increase the number of people engaged in meaningful employment, education or training when they leave school. These should include such actions as the following:

- make a concerted drive to lift the performances of students not currently succeeding in the education system;
- establish a Joint Committee comprising representatives of key ministries who are, or should be, involved in transition programmes to determine and oversee transition policies involving students at risk for NEET;
- review policies on technical and vocational education and training;
- create Transition Coaches in secondary schools;
- develop transition programmes in secondary schools targeting students from the age of 14 and taking particular account of the impact of disruptive technologies on the workplace;
- institute training programmes for secondary teachers and other personnel involved in implementing transition programmes;
- develop comprehensive work experiences for all secondary students;
- establish local Employment Committees targeting individuals most at risk for NEET; and
- review existing tertiary education programmes' effectiveness in working with NEET students.

See also **Strategies 21** and **29**.

Sources

Diversities in education, Chapter 6. Op cit.

OECD (2010). *Learning for jobs*. Paris. URL: www.oecd.org/edu/learningforjobs

Quintini, G., Martin, J.P & Martin, S. (2007). *The changing nature of the school-to-work transition process in OECD countries*. Bonn: Institute for the Study of Labor (IZA).

3

BUREAUCRACY

'Government proposes, bureaucracy disposes'

This quote from P.J. O'Rourke in the title nicely defines the role of bureaucracies in a democracy. Contrasting views are held about such bodies. These range from Joseph Schumpeter's view that 'Bureaucracy is not an obstacle to democracy, but an inevitable complement to it', to Laurence J. Peters' somewhat cynical description of a bureaucracy as 'defending the status quo long past the time when the quo has lost its status'.

More prosaically, a bureaucracy refers to both a body of non-elective government officials and an administrative policy-making group. In some countries they comprise 'ministries', in others, 'departments'. Depending on the political structure of countries, these entities may be present at the national level, the state or provincial level, or the district or municipality level, or all three.

Bureaucracies are primarily responsible for advising governments on policies and for implementing them. However, they usually also have delegated authority to develop policies and regulations, as long as these are in accord with those promulgated by their governments. These comprise the strategies outlined in this chapter.

Education bureaucracies have varying degrees of authority over schools, depending in part on the degree of devolution that exists in different countries. Thus, some are very centralized (e.g. France, Ireland and Slovenia), while others are very decentralized (e.g. USA, New Zealand, UK, Sweden, Norway, and Switzerland). The trend is towards decentralization (see European Agency for Special Needs and Inclusive Education, 2017).

Sources

European Agency for Special Needs and Inclusive Education (2017). *Decentralisation in education systems: Seminar report*. Odense, Denmark.
Schumpeter, J.A. (1942). *Capitalism, socialism and democracy*. Routledge (2003).
Peters, L.J. (1977). *Peters's quotations: Ideas for our time*. William Morrow.

Strategy 19: Avoid grade repetition

Rationale

Among OECD countries, in 2009, there was a large variation in students repeating grades at least once, as shown in the following figures (OECD, 2014):

Lowest 10 countries, in order: Iceland (0.9%), Slovenia (1.5%), UK (2.2%), Finland (2.8%), Slovak Republic (3.8%), Czech Republic (4.0%), Denmark (4.4%), Sweden (4.6%), and New Zealand (5.1%).

Highest 10 countries, in reverse order: France (36.9%), Luxembourg (36.5%), Spain (35.3%), Portugal (35.0%), Belgium (34.9%), Netherlands (26.7%), Chile (23.4%), Switzerland (22.8%), Mexico (21.5%) and Germany (21.4%).

The OECD average was 13%, close to the US figure of 14.2%.

John Hattie (2009) is very critical of grade repetition. Indeed, he pointed out that it is difficult to find any study showing a positive effect on student achievement. Rather, the trend is towards negative effects (d = −0.16) for grade retention. Further, he noted that research indicates that the threat of non-promotion does not motivate students to try harder; on the contrary, it is a de-motivating force, which increases the likelihood of students dropping out of school. Policies that help students stay on track academically have the potential not only to benefit students at risk for academic failure, but also to enhance the positive behaviour of other students in the grade.

According to an OECD study (Ikeda & García, 2014), in most countries examined, students who repeated a grade in secondary school tended to perform better than those who repeated a grade in primary school, but non-repeaters tended to perform even better than secondary-school repeaters. These findings remain unchanged, even after controlling for students' socio-economic background.

The strategy

Alternative strategies to reduce this practice include:

- preventing repetition by addressing learning gaps during the school year;
- automatic promotion (sometimes called 'social promotion');
- limiting repetition to subject or modules failed, with targeted support;
- raising awareness across schools and society about the impact of grade retention on students; and
- making governments aware of the financial costs of grade retention.

Governments may be well advised to investigate the policies that have led some countries to have very low rates of grade repetition.

Sources

Diversities in education, Chapter 3. Op cit.

Hattie, J. (2009). *Visible learning*. Routledge.

Ikeda, M., & García, E. (2014). 'Grade repetition: A comparative study of academic and non-academic consequences.' *OECD Journal: Economic Studies, 2013/1*. URL: http://dx.doi.org/10.1787/eco_ studies-2013-5k3w65mx3hnx

Strategy 20: Defer the specialized tracking of students to the age of 15–16 years

Rationale

There are three ways of selecting students according to ability:

1   ability grouping within mixed ability classes;
2   streaming, which involves allocating students to different classes based on their ability and/or achievement; and
3   tracking, which means providing different programmes, sometimes in different schools, for students according to their different abilities and interests (in the United States, 'tracking' usually refers to streaming).

The first two are discussed in **Strategy 36**; here I focus on the third.

The age at which students are separated into different tracks varies among countries. Germany and Switzerland, for example, have separate middle or lower secondary schools based largely on the school's assessment of a student's academic potential. Finland and Denmark, on the other hand, keep all students in a common, untracked comprehensive school up through grade 9 or 10, at which point students and their families decide which kind of upper secondary education they will pursue.

UNESCO and the ILO (International Labour Organization) favour the second of these two approaches. They state that premature and narrow specialization should be avoided: (a) in principle, the age of 15 should be considered the lower limit for beginning specialization; and (b) a period of common studies providing basic knowledge and generic skills should be required for each broad occupational sector before a special branch is chosen.

In a comprehensive study, Hanushek and Wößmann (2006) identified tracking effects on outcomes across tracked and non-tracked systems. Their results suggested that early tracking increases educational inequality and reduces mean performance. Further, the OECD noted that early student selection has a negative impact on students assigned to lower tracks and exacerbates inequalities, without raising average performance. It argued that student selection should be deferred to upper secondary education while reinforcing comprehensive schooling prior to that stage.

The strategy

Specialized tracking of students should occur no earlier than the age of 15-16 years. Before then, schools should be comprehensive in character.

See also **Strategies 18** and **21**.

Sources

Diversities in education, Chapter 3. Op cit.

Hanushek, E., & Wößmann, L. (2006). 'Does educational tracking affect performance and inequality? Differences-in-differences evidence across countries.' *Economic Journal, 116*(510), C63–C76.

OECD (2012). *Equity and quality in education: Supporting disadvantaged students and schools.* Paris.

UNESCO/ILO (2002). *Technical and vocational education and training for the twenty-first century: UNESCO and ILO recommendations.* Paris/Geneva.

Strategy 21: Design equivalent VET pathways for upper secondary education

Rationale

According to the OECD (2012) between 10 and 30% of 15–16 year-olds starting upper secondary education do not complete it. It recommended making academic and vocational pathways to upper secondary qualifications equivalent by improving the quality of vocational education and training (VET). This is already being done in a number of European countries. A US report advocated bringing that country's upper secondary school system more into line with European approaches (Symonds et al., 2011). Two features were emphasized. First, throughout northern and central Europe, where VET is a mainstream system, this pathway helps most young people make the transition from adolescence to productive adulthood. In 2010, some 50% of Europe's young people completed their education and entered the labour market via a VET path. Second, in Austria, Denmark, Finland, Germany, the Netherlands, Norway and Switzerland, after grades 9 or 10, between 40 and 70% of young people opted for educational programmes that typically combine classroom and workplace learning over the subsequent three years. This culminates in a diploma or certificate, with real currency in the labour market. In virtually all of these countries, VET also provides a pathway into tertiary education for those who choose to take it.

Similarly, in Australia, more than 90% of schools offer VET in Years 11 and 12 and all states and territories have introduced reforms to increase the number of students who participate in VET (Education Services Australia (2014).

The strategy

The essence of this strategy is to design VET pathways for upper secondary education of equivalent standing to academic pathways.

According to Education Services Australia (2014), such pathways should contribute to preparing skilled and flexible workers able to navigate the world of work, interact with others, plan and organize, make decisions, identify and solve problems, create and innovate and work in a digital world. They should also include work experience and structured work placements.

To bring this about, VET requires highly qualified teachers, trainers and guidance counsellors; innovative teaching methods; high-quality infrastructure and facilities; a high labour market relevance; the capacity to transfer between academic and vocational studies; and collaboration between schools and employers.

See also **Strategies 18** and **20**.

Sources

Education Services Australia (2014). *Preparing secondary students for work.*
OECD (2012). *Equity and quality in education: Supporting disadvantaged students and schools.* Paris.
Symonds, W.C., Schwartz, R.B., & Ferguson, R. (2011). *Pathways to prosperity: Meeting the challenge of preparing young Americans for the 21st century.* Cambridge, MA: Harvard Graduate School of Education.

Strategy 22: Reduce class size if accompanied by evidence-based measures

Rationale

Teachers and parents typically consider that smaller classes allow teachers to focus more on the needs of individual students. While this seems common sense, it is not automatic. As noted by OECD's Andreas Schleicher (2015), 'PISA results show no relationship between class size and learning outcomes, neither within nor across countries'. Further, as Hattie (2009) has pointed out, teachers in smaller classes tend to adopt the same teaching methods they use in larger classes and not take advantage of having fewer students. Unsurprisingly, in his synthesis of studies into reducing class size from 25 to 15 students, Hattie found a low effect size of 0.21.

On the other hand, some studies point to more positive outcomes. One example is the Student Teacher Achievement Ratio (or STAR) study conducted in Tennessee during the late 1980s (Finn, 2002). In this study, students and teachers were randomly assigned to small classes, with an average of 15 students, or regular classes, with an average of 22 students. It focused on class reduction and did not provide special training for teachers. This large reduction in class size was found to increase student achievement in reading and mathematics by an amount equivalent to about 3 additional months of schooling. Smaller classes appeared overall to benefit children with special needs, children from minority groups and younger children during the first years of school. The more years spent in reduced classes, the longer lasting the benefits.

Similar to the STAR findings, Blatchford (2003) and his colleagues in the United Kingdom found a clear effect of class size on children's academic attainment over the first year of school, in both literacy and mathematics. Also, small classes were particularly beneficial for disadvantaged pupils.

The strategy

In setting class sizes, serious consideration should be given to having fewer students in first 3–4 years of schooling and in classes with a high proportion of disadvantaged children.

If class sizes are lowered, teachers should be prepared to modify their pedagogy by incorporating evidence-based strategies.

Policy makers should carry out cost–benefit analyses, comparing lowering class sizes with other educational approaches.

Sources

Blatchford, P. (2003). *The class size debate: Is small better?* Maidenhead, UK: Open University Press.
Finn, J.D. (2002). 'Small classes in American schools: Research, practice and politics.' *Phi Delta Kappan*, March, 551–560.
Hattie, J. (2009). *Visible learning*. Routledge.
Schleicher, A. (2015). 'Seven big myths about top-performing school systems.' *BBC News*, 4 February 2015.
What really works, Chapter 25. Op cit.

Strategy 23: Collect disaggregated data on student achievement

Rationale

Data can be analyzed in two main ways. First, it can be aggregated, which involves collecting information from two or more sources and expressing it in a summary form. Second, data can be disaggregated, or extracted, from aggregated data. This involves delving more deeply into a set of results to highlight differences in such variables as age, gender, income, ethnicity or language. It helps to expose hidden trends and enables the identification of vulnerable populations. In the case of schools, it can help plan appropriate programmes, decide which interventions to select and direct limited resources to those who need it most.

Two examples of disaggregating data show its utility. First, in the United Kingdom, Strand (2014) focused on the intersections between ethnicity, gender and class. For example, at age 16, White British girls achieved better results than White British boys, a gender gap that was significantly larger among Bangladeshi and Black Caribbean students. When socio-economic status was added to the mix, the situation became even more complex. For example, among low SES boys, White British and Black Caribbean boys were jointly the lowest scoring groups. As Strand said, 'there is something about the particular combination of ethnicity, SES and gender that is uniquely related to attainment' (p. 133). Disaggregating achievement data allows such a conclusion to be drawn.

Second, United States' data showed that Asian children on average had relatively low rates of achieving less than a high school level education (14%) (Khan, & Ro, 2009). However, by disaggregating the data, differences within that population were revealed; specifically, among Hmong, Laotian and Cambodian populations, the rates were more than double the Asian average.

The strategy

Disaggregation of educational data is probably best undertaken at a system or school level, rather than at a class level where there is low statistical power related to small sample sizes. As a rule of thumb, data should not be disaggregated further than a cell size of 20.

The main data categories of relevance to education are age, gender, ethnicity and socio-economic status, with consideration being given to the intersection of these categories.

Sources

Diversities in education, Chapters 2 and 7. Op cit.

Khan, S, & Ro, M. (2009). *Disaggregation of data: Needs and challenges for collecting and reporting race/ethnicity data*. Webinar. URL: www.sharedaction.org/contentOnly/images/pdf/data_webinar_2009_0819.pdf

Strand, S. (2014). 'Ethnicity, gender, social class and achievement gaps at age 16: Intersectionality and "getting it" for the white working class.' *Research Papers in Education, 29*(2), 131–171.

Strategy 24: Ensure that the curriculum contains an historical perspective on oppression and inequality

Rationale

Students should have a sense of the history that underpins their own lives and current affairs, particularly those centring on gender, class, religion, race and disability. This should enable them to become more aware of their own identity and also to gain a greater appreciation of people who differ from themselves.

The strategy

Here are some of the negative aspects of countries' histories that should be incorporated in school curricula:

- religious persecution and conflict: e.g. Christian Crusades against Muslims during the 11th to 13th centuries; and the Wars of Religion, involving Protestants and Catholics, in the 16th and 17th centuries in Europe;
- gender discrimination: e.g. women's lack of access to higher education and delays in receiving the right to vote;
- social class exploitation: e.g. unfair labour laws;
- institutional racism: e.g. in the United States, the Chinese Exclusion Act of 1882 and the internment of Japanese during World War II;
- laws and regulations which led to racial segregation of residential areas: e.g. in the United States, the racial segregation of federally-funded public housing from the Franklin Roosevelt's New Deal, which was continued during and after World War II;
- discriminatory educational practices: e.g. slaves being forbidden to learn to read, Native American children being removed from their homes and placed in boarding schools and the outlawing of languages other than English; and
- segregation of people with disabilities: e.g. placement in psychiatric hospitals for life and denial of access to education.

On the positive side, students should also be taught about:

- the history, traditions, languages and cultures of minorities as well as majority groups;
- how, throughout history, religion has been a vital and pervasive feature of human life;
- the struggles against racism and discrimination, as epitomized by Martin Luther King;
- the work of the United Nations in advocating for human rights; and
- the history of other countries and cultures, as well as how others have looked at the students' own society.

In this entire endeavour, educators must ensure that history teaching is not an instrument of ideological manipulation, of propaganda or is used for the promotion of intolerant and ultra-nationalistic, xenophobic, racist or anti-Semitic ideas.

Source

Diversities in education, Chapters 2–6. Op cit.

Strategy 25: Avoid ethnic disproportionality in special education placements

Rationale

Disproportionality refers to the representation of a particular group of students at a rate different than that found in the general population. For example, in the United States, special education statistics have shown that, compared with their presence in the general population, Black students were considerably over-represented in 10 of the 13 disability categories by up to twice their national population estimates. Conversely, there is clear evidence they were under-represented in gifted programmes relative to White students. For example, in 2009, Black students constituted 16.7% of the student population but just 9.8% of students in gifted programmes.

Similar disproportionality has been noted within the United Kingdom where in England Travellers of Irish heritage and Gypsy/ Roma students were disproportionately classified as having special educational needs. There were differences in particular categories; for example, Black Caribbean and Mixed White and Black Caribbean pupils were 1.5 times more likely to be identified as having behavioural, emotional and social difficulties than White British pupils.

Against these trends in the United States and England, in New Zealand the ethnic distribution of children classified as having high or very high needs matched that of the general school population. They are, however, over-represented among students with behavioural issues.

Ethnic disproportionality is generally seen as a serious matter. Writers have noted that misclassification in special education programmes can result in (a) a child's removal from the regular education setting, (b) the likelihood of encountering a limited curriculum, (c) lower teacher expectations and (d) poor post-school outcomes. Conversely, children who are wrongly determined as not requiring special education miss out on additional support.

Just a word of caution: some writers argue that social class, rather than ethnicity, may be the more significant variable to focus on when considering over-representation.

The strategy

What are some of the possible explanations for ethnic disproportionality? These can include such factors as (a) the lack of congruence between minority cultures and school cultures, (b) the legacy of deficit thinking about racial minorities, (c) the history of school racial segregation (at least in the United States), (d) resource inequalities, (e) asynchronous power relationships between school authorities and minority parents, (f) culturally inappropriate or insensitive pedagogy and assessment practices and (g) inadequate professional development for teachers. All these should be addressed.

As well, education authorities should identify disproportionality in special education placements across disability categories and take action to address any disproportionality.

Source

Diversities in education, Chapter 4. Op cit.

Strategy 26: Avoid gender disproportionality in special education placements

Rationale

Abundant evidence shows significant gender differences in access to special education. For example, in the United States, since the 1960s, the overall male to female ratio in special education has been between 2:1 and 3:1. Within the United Kingdom, according to recent studies, 68% of students in special schools in England were boys, and almost five times as many boys as girls are expelled from school. The OECD, too, has reported gender imbalances in special education enrolments across a range of countries.

At least part of the over-representation of boys in special education can be attributed to the preponderance of boys over girls in the incidence of disabilities. For only a few childhood disorders are prevalence rates higher for girls than boys. These include separation anxiety, selective mutism, neural tube defects and translocation Down syndrome. For all other impairments or disabilities, males predominate: for example, trisomic Down syndrome (59% males), speech impairment (60%), learning disabilities (73%), and emotional disorders (76%). There is also evidence that boys are more likely to be diagnosed with ADHD (attention deficit hyperactivity disorder) than girls.

As I noted in **Strategy 23**, gender interacts with ethnicity and socio-economic status to influence students' achievement. As mentioned, this was shown in a UK study of achievement at age 16, where White British girls did better than White British boys, a gender gap that was significantly larger among Bangladeshi and Black Caribbean students.

Some writers argue that these gender imbalances reflect either or both an over-identification of males and an under-identification of girls. Also, at least one writer has interpreted the gender imbalance to mean that boys receive more resources than girls and thus unfairly gain more access to the curriculum. According to this argument, it would therefore be ironic were over-representation of boys considered to be a problem for them.

The strategy

It must be recognized that, to some extent, gender imbalances in the incidence of low achievement and behavioural problems reflect biological factors, which may await advances in medical research.

They may also reflect educators and associated professions over-identifying boys as having behavioural problems and, conversely, under-identifying girls with less overt behaviour problems.

For both boys and girls, the goal should be to improve achievement and behaviour by implementing strategies such as those outlined in this book.

Source

Diversities in education, Chapters 2 and 6. Op cit.

Strategy 27: Implement intercultural education

Rationale

There are three contrasting approaches to schools' accommodation to cultural diversity. The first of these is *assimilation*, when schools teach students to become citizens of a 'melting pot' state. Effectively, this means ethnic minorities having their cultural identities suppressed in favour of the majority culture. The second approach is *multiculturalism*, which has been variously interpreted. At its most extreme, it equates to an education system that leads to an aggregation of diverse monocultural schools with students grouped largely on the basis of their ethnicity. Multiculturalism has been increasingly criticized as fostering communal segregation and mutual incomprehension, or what Amartya Sen (2006) has called 'plural mono-culturalism'. The third approach is *interculturalism*, defined by UNESCO (2005) as 'the existence and equitable interaction of diverse cultures and the possibility of generating shared cultural expressions through dialogue and mutual respect' (Article 8).

The strategy

According to the Council of Europe (2008), intercultural education comprises 'an open and respectful exchange of views between individuals, groups with different ethnic, cultural, religious and linguistic backgrounds and heritage on the basis of mutual understanding and respect' (p. 10).

UNESCO considers that intercultural education should:

- respect the cultural identity of learners through the provision of culturally appropriate and responsive quality education for all;
- provide all learners with the cultural knowledge, attitudes and skills necessary to achieve active and full participation in society; and
- provide all learners with cultural knowledge, attitudes and skills that enable them to contribute to respect, understanding and solidarity among individuals, ethnic, social, cultural and religious groups and nations.

Further, the Council of Europe recommends:

- using examples and content from a variety of cultures to illustrate key concepts in subjects;
- imparting knowledge about the history, traditions, languages and cultures of minorities to majority groups and about society as a whole to minorities;
- developing a critical awareness of the struggles against racism and discrimination;
- acquiring knowledge about students' own cultural heritages;
- developing an awareness of the increasing global interdependence between peoples and nations; and
- encouraging students to reflect critically on their own responses and attitudes to other cultures.

Sources

Council of Europe (2008). *Living together as equals in dignity*. White Paper on intercultural dialogue. Strasbourg.
Diversities in education, Chapter 4. Op cit.
Sen, A. (2006). 'The uses and abuses of multiculturalism.' *New Republic*, 27 February 2006.
UNESCO (2005). *Convention on the Protection and Promotion of the Diversity of Cultural Expressions*. Paris.

Strategy 28: Develop a religious and moral education curriculum

Rationale

Most western societies are becoming increasingly religiously diverse and more and more people claim they adhere to no religion. This does not mean that religion should not be taught in schools, but rather that a single religion should not be part of the school curriculum. Rather, the school curriculum should include:

- consideration of alternative worldviews;
- critical questioning, as opposed to indoctrination;
- the absence of distortion of any religion or belief;
- moral education; and
- cognizance of children's levels of cognitive maturity.

These principles should not be interpreted as denying the right of individuals to adopt a religion or belief of their choice, as specified in the UN's *Covenant on Civil and Political Rights*. Nor do they deny the rights of parents or legal guardians to ensure the religious and moral education of their children in conformity with their own convictions – but outside the school context. They also rest on the right of the child to freedom of thought, conscience and religion, as specified in Article 14(1) of the *Convention on the Rights of the Child*. This *Convention* acknowledges the rights of parents and legal guardians to provide direction to the child, but in a manner consistent with the evolving capacities of the child.

The strategy

The strategy I am advocating could be described as 'plural religious education'. Essentially, it requires that students learn about the basic practices, beliefs, rituals etc. of a variety of religions. They are presented with information about these religious traditions but are not taught that any are (un)true. This should also extend to philosophies and beliefs of a non-religious nature. Let me emphasize: this is *not* religious instruction in a single faith, which I equate with indoctrination.

Such religious education could well include, or be extended to cover, moral education. At its heart is conceptual analysis and thinking critically and independently about moral issues, including religious questions. It could also incorporate Ethics, with the goal of helping students grow into independent, tolerant, responsible and judicious members of a democratic society.

An extension of this approach is the teaching of 'Philosophy for Children'. This typically involves a teacher presenting a thought-provoking stimulus, around which students frame philosophical questions, with the teacher engaging in a Socratic dialogue with them. At its heart is thinking critically and independently about moral issues, including religious questions.

See also **Strategies 45** and **47**.

Source

. *Diversities in education*, Chapter 5. Op cit.

4

COMMUNITIES

Making connections

The *Oxford Dictionary* quite simply defines a community as 'A group of people living in the same place or having a particular characteristic in common.'

There are three main types of communities relevant to schools:

1   *Proximal communities*: these comprise the staff members who work in a school, the students and their immediate families/caregivers, the school governing body, the parent–teacher association, and local residents and organizations with a stake in the school.
2   *Distal communities*: these extend beyond the immediate vicinity of a school and include regional or district bodies such as teacher unions, employer organizations and cultural bodies. They also include recent developments in *communities of learning*, or *communities of practice*. In New Zealand, these comprise groups of schools that come together, along with their communities, to raise achievement for all students by sharing expertise in teaching and learning, and supporting each other. They also facilitate stronger transitions into, between and out of different levels of schooling (Ministry of Education, 2016).
3   *Virtual communities*: these comprise social networks of individuals who interact via the Internet in order to pursue mutual interests or goals. They may be drawn from either proximal or distal communities, the latter crossing geographical boundaries, even with global connections.

Zoning is a critical issue related to school communities. This concerns students' eligibility to enroll in particular schools. In some jurisdictions, students may only be enrolled in their local neighbourhood school, restricted to a delineated geographic area. In others, there is open enrollment, with parents able to exercise choice as to which school their child attends. I take up this matter in **Strategies 5** and **25**. I am particularly concerned at how school zoning impacts on the degree of SES and ethnic mix in schools.

Another issue is the extent to which communities exercise power in the governance and management of schools. In some locations, communities have very little input into schools, with most of the power being vested in the schools themselves or in higher authorities. In others, communities have considerable authority. In my own country New Zealand, for example, parents elect schools' governing bodies ('boards of trustees'), which have responsibility for appointing staff, determining budget allocations and ensuring compliance with regulations.

Sources

Ministry of Education (2016). *Community of learning: Guide for schools and kura*. Wellington. URL: https://education.govt.nz/assets/Documents/Ministry/Investing-in-Educational-Success/Communities-of-Schools/Communities-of-Learning-Guide-for-Schools-and-Kura-web-enabled.pdf

Strategy 29: Link schools with their distal communities

Rationale

The traditional borders between schools and their communities are undergoing dramatic change. There are many drivers of this change, but the most significant one is probably the realization that not only should schools cooperate with each other, but also that education and related services must work together, rather than be in competition with each other.

There is a whole range of working relationships that schools and other organizations can have with one another (Community Toolbox). Four in particular stand out: (1) *networking*, when they exchange information in order to help each other do a better job; (2) *coordinating*, when they modify their activities so that, together, they provide better services to their constituents; (3) *cooperating*, when they not only share information and make adjustments in their services, but share resources to help each other do a better job; and (4) *collaborating*, when they help each expand or enhance their capacities to do their jobs, in a spirit of partnership. These relationships require a progressively greater investment of time and trust. Also, to a greater or lesser extent, technical, organizational, political barriers, and just plain inertia can limit their implementation. But there is a growing recognition that the whole is greater than the sum of its parts.

The strategy

In this strategy, I will examine three relationships between schools and their distal communities, with a focus on professional entities. All three should be implementing the collaborative model.

> *Wraparound services.* Increasingly, since the 1990s or so, there has been a distinct trend towards 'joined-up thinking' in providing human services. This reflects a recognition that the challenge of educating children with special educational needs is essentially a multi-disciplinary enterprise, requiring the highest possible levels of collaboration among services. It means dismantling 'silos' or, at the very least, avoiding 'silo thinking' in which professionals or agencies compete rather than cooperate. See also **Strategy 3**.

> *Full-service schools.* In a nutshell, a full-service school is a 'one-stop' institution that integrates education, medical, social and/or human services to meet the needs of children and youth and their families in a single campus.

> *Communities of learning.* These comprise clusters of schools that come together to raise achievement for all students by sharing expertise in teaching and learning, and by supporting each other. They also facilitate stronger transitions into, between and out of different levels of schooling.

Sources

Community Toolbox URL: http://ctb.ku.edu/en/table-of-contents/implement/improving-services/
  coordination-cooperation-collaboration/main
Diversities in education, Chapter 3. Op cit.
What really works, Chapter 26. Op cit.

Strategy 30: Recognize that inclusion is a community matter

Rationale

Inclusion goes beyond the school gates and should include the broader community, both during compulsory schooling and beyond into adulthood. Indeed, it should be a lifelong process. At the heart of inclusion is developing a sense of belonging in a family, in a community, in a society. It means being valued as a person.

The UN *Convention on the Rights of Persons with Disabilities* makes it clear that people with a disability have a right to 'full and effective participation in society on an equal basis with others'. This implies that all people, regardless of their abilities or disabilities, have the right to:

- be respected as full members of their communities;
- participate in leisure and recreational activities;
- enter into relationships with partners;
- work at jobs with competitive wages;
- travel using their own or public transport;
- associate freely with families and friends;
- join a church of their choosing;
- participate in cultural activities in keeping with their cultural identities;
- have full access to appropriate further education;
- join clubs and groups with others who share similar interests;
- have their needs taken fully into account in situations of armed conflict and natural disasters; and
- enjoy access to virtual communities through the Internet.

The strategy

To be able to enjoy these rights and attain the best quality of life possible, persons with disabilities need to (a) be prepared in inclusive education programmes at school (see **Strategy 15**); (b) have access to tailored transition programmes (see also **Strategy 18**) (Mitchell , 2015); (c) have ongoing access to appropriate post-school education and mentoring (ibid.); and (d) have access to wraparound services when required (see **Strategy 3**). As well, governments should strengthen their statistical capacity to produce reliable disaggregated data on persons with disabilities in order to support the design and the monitoring of better policies and programmes for them (see **Strategy 23**).

Barriers to the implementation of these recommendations should be addressed. These include the funding of services, persons with disabilities and their caregivers; the underestimation of the competence and needs of persons with disabilities; and, in some countries, stigma and shame associated with such persons.

Sources

Mitchell, D. (2015). 'What's next? Standards and guidelines for strengthening school-to-post-school transition programmes for students with disabilities.' In D.L. Cameron, & R. Thygesen (eds), *Transitions in the field of special education: Theoretical perspectives and implications for practice* (pp. 271–297). Munster and New York: Waxman.

5

SCHOOLS

Learning organizations with permeable borders

Traditionally, schools have been defined as institutions designed to provide learning environments (classrooms) for the teaching of children and adolescents under the direction of teachers, following a set curriculum. They may be public or private institutions. Public schools have legal obligations to adhere to policies determined by the relevant bodies at local and national levels, a relationship that sometimes leads to tensions. Private schools enjoy greater autonomy, but are more subject to market forces.

In recent years, schools have been undergoing two main changes:

1   School borders are becoming more permeable. Thus, we are seeing these borders undergoing considerable changes between:

- schools: there is a growing trend for schools to enter into collaborative arrangements with each other (see **Strategy 29**);
- schools and their communities: in many countries, parents are playing an increasingly active role in school governance and becoming directly involved in their children's education (see **Strategy 73**);
- education and work: schools are increasingly aware of their responsibility to prepare students for the world of work and therefore to make collaborative connections with employers (see **Strategy 18**);
- education and broader social responsibilities: for example, some schools are collaborating with various social and health agencies in shared campuses (see **Strategy 29**);
- formal and informal education;
- teachers and learners: teachers are transitioning from being 'sages on the stage' to 'guides on the side'; and
- the real world and the virtual world: students are increasingly relying on the Internet for supplementing, even replacing, classroom education (see **Strategies 39** and **66**).

2   Schools are increasingly being defined as learning organizations. For example, a recent OECD (2016) paper proposes a model of schools as learning organizations that focuses on:

- developing and sharing a vision centred on the learning of all students;
- creating and supporting continuous learning opportunities for all staff;
- promoting team learning and collaboration among all staff (see **Strategy 40**);

- establishing a culture of inquiry, innovation and exploration;
- embedding systems for collecting and exchanging knowledge and learning;
- learning with and from the external environment and larger learning systems; and
- modelling and growing learning leadership (see **Strategy 78**).

In short, schools as learning organizations have the capacity to change and adapt to new environments and circumstances as their members, individually and together, learn their way to realising their vision (OECD, 2016).

Sources

OECD (2016). *What makes a school a learning organisation? A guide for policy makers, school leaders and teachers*. Paris.

Strategy 31: Monitor developments in the implications of neuroscience for education

Rationale

The brain, with its 100 billion nerve cells, is the seat of our mental faculties, performing such higher functions as language, reasoning and memory. If, for any reason, any component of the brain is not functioning optimally, a person's capacity to learn will be affected. Neuroscience is giving us fruitful leads to follow, a situation that will undoubtedly improve in the future. We already know a great deal about seven key principles:

1 The brain is divided into different areas, each of which is closely associated with specific *functions*. For example, the forebrain is the home of our intellectual activities – memories, executive system, imagination, reasoning and thinking; the parietal lobes are responsible for integrating sensory information, linking language to memory and determining spatial sense; and the hippocampus sends memories out to the appropriate part of the brain for long-term storage and retrieval when required.

2 The developing brain is incredibly plastic and adaptable. Neighbouring and connected parts of it are able to assume some or most of the functions of damaged or malfunctioning areas. This is relevant to **Strategy 52**, Universal Design for Learning, in which learners are provided with multiple ways of learning and demonstrating their knowledge.

3 'Neurons that fire together, wire together'. Synapses between two neurons are strengthened if frequent connections are made. This draws attention to the importance of review and practice (**Strategy 61**).

4 'Use it or lose it'. The main function of a neuron is to connect with other neurons, either close by or at greater distances. Unless this happens, it will be removed.

5 There are 'sensitive periods' when certain types of learning are optimal. For example, for sensory stimuli such as speech sounds and for certain emotional and language experiences, there are relatively tight sensitive periods – hence the importance of early intervention (**Strategy 7**).

6 Emotions are part of the brain's ability to process information and regulate behaviour. We remember events that are charged with positive emotion, while too much emotion can make us irrational and undiscriminating. See **Strategy 57** on enhancing students' social and emotional learning.

7 The brain is a meaning-maker. This is illustrated in children's ability to make sense of their linguistic environment and to intuitively develop the grammar of the language(s) to which they are exposed. Of course, they require a good deal of quality experiences to be able to do so (see **Strategies 10, 14** and **58**).

Source

What really works, Chapters 2 and 11. Op cit.

Strategy 32: Examine what kind of masculinities are being promoted in the school

Rationale

More boys than girls exhibit behaviour patterns such as disregard for authority and low motivation for academic work. A New Zealand study found that females scored better than males on standardized tests of achievement and achieved more school and post-school qualifications (Gibb et al., 2008). These differences could not be explained by differences in cognitive ability as both genders had similar IQ scores. However, from age 6 to age 12, compared with girls, boys were described by their teachers as displaying significantly higher levels of distractible, restless, inattentive, aggressive, anti-social and oppositional behaviour. When the scores were adjusted for gender differences in these behaviours, most of the achievement differences were eliminated.

One of the crucial factors leading to these behaviours among boys is the importance for many of them of being accepted by other boys, to enable them to identify with and act in line with peer group norms, so they are seen as *belonging*, rather than as *different*. In many western countries, such acceptance is often dependent on showing behaviours such as I outlined above. These behaviours, along with speech, dress and body language seem to make up a pattern of 'laddishness' and risk-taking aimed at gaining and protecting a macho image. Such laddishness often runs counter to the expectations of the school and poses challenges for school personnel.

The strategy

Schools should examine their policies and teachers their behaviours to determine the extent to which they consciously or unconsciously promote stereotyped images of what it is to be a male or a female and how they should interact. This means, for example, dealing with such masculinized issues as 'laddish' behaviour, bullying of gays and attention-seeking.

Educators therefore have to ask themselves what constitutes acceptable masculine behaviours and how these can be promoted. It is much easier to define what is *not* acceptable than what *is* acceptable. This challenge becomes even greater when consideration is given to the rights and needs of LGBT students.

The only thing I can say with certainty is that while there is wide agreement as to what constitutes unacceptable behavior among males, there is no single template for what constitutes acceptable masculinity and schools would be wise to accept this.

See also **Strategy 35**.

Sources

Diversities in education, Chapter 2. Op cit.

Gibb, S.J., Fergusson, D.M., & Horwood, L.J. (2008). 'Gender differences in educational achievement to age 25.' *Australian Journal of Education, 52*(1), 63–80.

Strategy 33: Recognize that children and young people have a right to sexuality education

Rationale

The World Health Organization (2003) articulated this right to sexuality education in the following terms:

> All persons, free of coercion, discrimination and violence have the right to: the highest attainable standard of health in relation to sexuality, including access to sexual and repro-ductive health care services; seek, receive and impart information in relation to sexuality; sexuality education; respect for bodily integrity; choice of partner; decide to be sexually active or not; consensual sexual relations; consensual marriage; decide whether or not, and when to have children; and to pursue a satisfying, safe and pleasurable sexual life.

The strategy

At the risk of seeming parochial, I am going to quote from the New Zealand Curriculum as a good example of a sexuality education programme. Here are the key features:

- Sexuality education is one of the key areas of learning and must be included in teaching programmes at both primary and secondary school levels.
- It provides students with the knowledge, understanding and skills to develop positive attitudes towards sexuality, to take care of their sexual health and to enhance their interpersonal relationships.
- Students will consider how the physical, social, mental and emotional and spiritual dimensions of sexuality influence their well-being.
- Students will critically examine the social, economic, political and cultural influences that shape the ways people learn about and express their sexuality. These influences may include gender roles, body image, discrimination, equity, mass media, social media in online environments, culturally-based values and beliefs and the law.
- Students require a range of developmentally appropriate learning opportunities in sex-uality education. For example, these include opportunities to develop:

  o knowledge, understandings and skills relating to sexual health and development: physical, emotional, mental, social and spiritual;
  o knowledge, understandings and skills to enhance their sexual and reproductive health, for example, knowledge about the process of conception and contraception;
  o understandings and skills to enhance relationships, for example in relation to friendships, intimate relationships, love, families and parenting; and
  o critical thinking, reflection and social-action skills related to issues of equity, gender, body image, sexualisation, risk and safety.

Sources

Diversities in education, Chapter 2. Op cit.

Ministry of Education (nd). Sexuality education in the New Zealand Curriculum. Wellington.

World Health Organization (2003). UN Commission on Human Rights Agenda item 6, Racism, Racial Discrimination, Xenophobia, and all Forms of Discrimination. Statement by the World Health Organization, Geneva, 24 March 2003.

Strategy 34: Make schools safe and inclusive for both genders and all sexual orientations

Rationale

Unfortunately, not all schools are safe places for some students, especially girls and those who are lesbian, gay, bisexual or transgender (LGBT).

Gender-based violence is a global phenomenon that knows no geographical, cultural, social, economic, ethnic or other boundaries. It disproportionately affects girls and women and is a major obstacle to gender equality. For example, a US survey of adults found that one in three girls and one in seven boys had been sexually abused at some point in their childhood, while another found that 75% of juvenile victims of Internet predators were girls. As I noted in **Strategy 10**, data from low- and middle-income countries paint an even worse picture, with up to 10% of adolescent girls reporting incidents of forced sexual intercourse or other sexual acts in the previous year, sometimes with teachers.

There is clear evidence, too, that LGBT students are disproportionately bullied at school and more likely to attempt suicide and experience significant depressive symptoms than their heterosexual peers. In the United States, for example, gay and lesbian teens are two to three times more likely to commit suicide than other youth. LGBT students report being five times more likely to miss school because they feel unsafe after being bullied due to their sexual orientation. Some feel forced to drop out of school altogether.

The strategy

Schools have a major responsibility to ensure that classrooms are made safe and inclusive for both genders and all sexual orientations. In fulfilling these responsibilities, teachers set the tone in their classrooms and school leaders influence the climate throughout a school.

In order respond to gender-based violence, governments should establish a monitoring framework with standardized indicators to establish the extent of school-related gender-based violence. Addressing such violence requires a multi-sectoral approach involving education, health, social welfare and youth sectors. School authorities should be vigilant in detecting, preventing and dealing with gender-based violence, both in school precincts and during students' travel to and from school.

Educators should anticipate that some LGBT students will have already 'come out', or would like to, and they should therefore be prepared to deal with their own reactions and those of the other students. They should also consider ways to include LGBT issues and themes in the curriculum (see **Strategies 24** and **33**). It is important that schools not become 'heteronormalizing institutions' and treat LGBT students as though they were invisible.

Source

Diversities in education, Chapter 2. Op cit.

Strategy 35: Avoid stereotyped gendered behaviour patterns

Rationale

Teachers and parents may hold various stereotypes regarding gender differences and explicitly or implicitly convey these to children in their care. Thus, for example, messages are conveyed that 'Boys are good at mathematics' or, conversely, that 'Girls are bad at mathematics'. Such messages that a particular subject is not important, useful, doable or part of their identity can have the effect of becoming self-fulfilling prophecies that influence the way children perform on particular tasks. There is a risk that stereotypes come to be believed and not challenged.

Although there are many examples of gender differences in general, three things must be remembered. First, many of them are quite small. Second, for almost every variable there is a high degree of overlap between genders. Third, there is greater diversity within genders than between them. It therefore behoves educators (and parents) to not impose gender stereotypes on their students.

The strategy

Schools represent the most direct policy levers with which to address negative gender stereotypes through individual guidance and encouragement, teacher expectations and teacher–student interactions.

Schools should regularly monitor students' progress, behaviour, attendance and exclusion by gender. Where patterns emerge that indicate one gender is cause for concern, steps should be taken to investigate further and take remedial action. This could include ensuring that the curriculum and teaching materials are free of gender-stereotyped imagery and gender bias.

The role of families in engendering gender stereotypes cannot be under-estimated. Parents can consciously or unconsciously teach their children about gender through the selection of toys, clothes, activities and the styles of play and emotional expression they encourage. Conventional gender expectations seem to be deeply entrenched, even when parents try to avoid them. Teachers can and should play a significant role in influencing parents to avoid gender stereotyping their children.

See also **Strategy 32**, in which I focus on stereotypes of masculinities and draw attention to the role of the peer group in constructing them.

Source

Diversities in education, Chapter 2. Op cit.

Strategy 36: Avoid streaming and ability grouping

Rationale

There are three ways of selecting students according to ability:

1   ability grouping within mixed ability classes;
2   streaming, which involves allocating students to different classes based on ability and/ or achievement (in the United States, this is usually referred to as 'tracking');
3   tracking, which means providing different programmes, sometimes in different schools, for students according to their different abilities and interests.

Here I focus on the first two, while the third was discussed in **Strategy 20**.

The literature provides a range of arguments as to why ability grouping is detrimental to low-achieving learners:

- being assigned to low-ability classes communicates low expectations to them, which might prove self-fulfilling;
- because ability grouping often parallels social class and ethnic groupings, it may increase divisions along class and ethnic lines;
- low-achieving learners tend to receive less instruction when placed in low-ability classes than when placed in mixed ability classes;
- classes composed solely of low-achieving learners do not provide a stimulating learning environment and lack positive role models;
- low-ability classes are much more likely to receive course content that focuses on below-grade level knowledge and skills than high-ability classes;
- students in higher tracks often have more effective teachers;
- students in lower tracks are often in classes where there are more disruptions;
- teachers of lower tracks have lower expectations of their students.

Typical of research on this topic is Hattie's (2009) report on 14 meta-analyses of ability grouping, which yielded a low effect size of 0.12. He concluded that 'tracking has minimal effects on learning outcomes and profound negative equity effects' (p. 90), with low-track students becoming more alienated, facing fewer intellectual challenges and less engaged in learning.

Notwithstanding this evidence, ability grouping is still widely employed in the United Kingdom, where, as of 2011, nearly 20% of children were separated into streams by the age of seven. Similarly, in the United States, 'tracking' in various forms has been among the predominant organizing practices in public schools for the last century, although 'de-tracking' has gained increasing favour in recent years. In contrast, Finland abolished streaming in 1985.

The strategy

The converse of avoiding streaming and ability grouping is, of course, favouring mixed ability grouping, both between and within classes. That is not to say that there is no place for some ability grouping within classes, which could be employed on occasion, as long as it is not the norm.

Sources

Hattie, J. (2009). *Visible learning*. Routledge.
What really works, Chapter 3. Op cit.

Strategy 37: Develop a supportive school culture

Rationale

Increasingly, attention is being paid to how the school as a unique organization impacts on the behaviour and achievement of its students. This notion draws our attention to a school's culture (sometimes referred to as a school's climate) and the way in which it both determines and reflects how its members behave towards each other: in classrooms, in playgrounds, in staffrooms and even in the community – anywhere where members of the school community meet each other.

The OECD has listed it as one of its top five recommendations for improving the achievement of low-SES students. If they are to be successful in introducing new ideas, school leaders have to work on changing the culture of their school.

School culture is closely linked with classroom climate (**Strategy 69**), but it is more than the aggregate of each classroom's climate, for the whole is greater than the sum of its parts. Creating a positive school culture involves developing and implementing goals for the school as a whole. These goals will reflect the shared values, beliefs, attitudes, traditions and behavioural norms of its members, particularly those in leadership positions. Change agents have to work on changing the culture of a school if they are to be successful in introducing new ideas.

The strategy

Those attributes of school culture that contribute positively to student performance include the following:

- a relentless focus on success for each and every student and on their well-being;
- positive teacher–student relationships;
- use of data information systems to identify struggling students and intervene early (see also **Strategy 23**);
- adequate and timely support such as counselling and mentoring;
- a strong commitment to accepting and celebrating diversity;
- a sensitivity to cultural issues (se also **Strategy 70**);
- high, but realistic, standards (see **Strategy 53**);
- strong connections with parents, including involvement in their children's learning (see also **Strategy 73**);
- a balance between trusting teachers to perform their duties and verifying their work;
- recognition of those who make positive contributions to the school culture;
- equitable distribution of resources;
- provision of instructional leadership;
- an atmosphere of innovation;
- high involvement of teachers in the decision-making process; and
- consideration of alternative ways of organizing instruction time over the day, week or year.

Sources

Diversities in education, Chapter 3. Op cit.
OECD (2012). *Equity and quality in education: Supporting disadvantaged students and schools*. Paris.
What really works, Chapter 25. Op cit.

Strategy 38: Implement School-Wide Positive Behaviour Support programmes

Rationale

School-Wide Positive Behaviour Support (SW-PBS) is a proactive approach to building a school's capacity to deal with behavioural challenges. It emphasizes (a) the prevention and reduction of chronic problem behaviour, (b) active instruction of adaptive skills, (c) a continuum of consequences for problem behaviours and (d) interventions for learners with the most intractable behaviours. It centres on the school as an organization.

The strategy

SW-PBS has four main elements:

1   *A team-based systems approach.* SW-PBS requires all members of the school staff to work together on a common agenda of goals and approaches to learners' behaviour. To achieve this, several factors are very important: school leadership, administrative support, on-site professional development for staff and consistency across all staff members.

2   *A proactive focus on prevention.* Within this theme, a three-tiered approach is taken:

    a   Primary prevention has the goal of creating a positive social culture and preventing new cases of problem behaviour from occurring. It involves all learners and adults within a school. It does not require individual learners to be identified.

    b   Secondary prevention is aimed at identifying and supporting individual learners at risk of engaging in more serious problem behaviour before they reach that stage.

    c   Tertiary prevention focuses on the smaller number of learners who engage in serious and chronic problem behaviour and require intensive, individualized intervention. See also **Strategy 44**.

3   *Evidence-based intervention.* There are two aspects to this. First, it is important that intervention strategies be based on the best available research evidence (**Strategy 2**). Second, decisions made on the implementation of SW-PBS, and any adjustments to it, should be based on data obtained from observations and interviews/ discussions within the school.

4   *Social skills instruction.* There are three main procedures for teaching pro-social behaviour (see also **Strategy 56**):

    a   Convey clear expectations by clearly defining and explaining what constitutes unacceptable behaviour and its consequences, as well as explaining and teaching about the school's expectations for positive social behaviours.

    b   Reinforce appropriate behaviour. This requires educators to identify appropriate behaviours when they occur in various locations in the school, to identify suitable rewards and to ensure they are delivered.

    c   Provide corrective consequences for inappropriate behaviour. Learners who perform inappropriate behaviour should receive a consequence, which could involve a verbal reprimand, a detention or referral to a senior staff member with responsibility for school discipline.

Source

What really works, Chapter 25. Op cit.

Strategy 39: Utilize information and communications technology

Rationale

A recent review (Escueta et al., 2017) pointed out that there is seemingly an endless array of information and communications technologies (ICT) from which to choose – from digital personalized learning platforms to educational games to online courses. Moreover, emerging fields like machine learning, big data and artificial intelligence will likely compound the influence of these technologies. Collectively, they offer the potential to expand access to quality education.

Advances in ICT mean that, at best, some jobs are likely to continue to be available but undergo significant transformations, whereas, at worst, some are likely to disappear altogether (perhaps 40% in the next 20 years). Routine tasks that are easily programmable and non-person-to-person interactions are most affected. These technological trends are therefore likely to impact most heavily on those who leave school with minimal or low qualifications, typically from low socio-economic homes, some ethnic minorities and those with disabilities.

Not all children are in a position to benefit from ICT. Many are on the wrong side of the 'digital divide', whether because their families or schools cannot afford modern technologies or their parents and teachers are unfamiliar with their use. Better-off, more educated households are most likely to provide their children with access.

The strategy

In order to maximize the impact of ICT, educators should:

> *Investigate the merits of Computer Assisted Learning (CAL).* There is a plethora of CAL products on the market, some of which show considerable promise in improving learning outcomes. Decisions on whether to pursue CAL and which programmes to use should be based on hard evidence.

> *Prepare students for a workforce that is increasingly transformed by ICT.*

> *Implement ICT access policies.* Schools and their governing authorities should aim for one-to-one computer access, particularly for students from low-SES homes.

> *Utilize ICT to enable collaborative teaching and professional learning.*

> *Utilize ICT to enable personalized learning.* CAL programmes can help to personalize learning by providing students with immediate feedback and teachers with rapid and regular data (see **Strategy 75**).

> *Use ICT to communicate personalized messages to students and their parents.* 'Nudge campaigns' can guide, encourage, or remind participants about their obligations.

> *Develop and/or access online courses.* These have come to constitute a sizeable presence within education, especially at the tertiary level. They are increasingly being accessed in the compulsory school sector.

See also **Strategies 18** and **66**.

Sources

Diversities in education, Chapters 1, 3 and 7. Op cit.

Escueta, M., Quan, V. Nickow, A.J., & Oreopoulos, P. (2017). *Education technology: An evidence-based review.* Cambridge, MA: National Bureau of Economic Research.

Strategy 40: Employ collaborative teaching

Rationale

As I pointed out in the introduction to this chapter, teaching is increasingly seen as a collaborative enterprise, where teachers and other professionals work alongside each other in shared teaching spaces. This has long been the case in inclusive education settings where teachers enjoy ongoing support from teaching assistants/paraprofessionals and periodic support and guidance from specialist teachers, medical specialists, therapists and others. Instead of being soloists, teachers have now become members of an orchestra.

Collaboration has the potential to provide opportunities for educators to learn from each other and thus reduce the professional isolation that can often occur in teaching. I recognize that if teachers have been used to working alone, it is a big step to develop new ways of working in which responsibilities and expertise are shared with other professionals, sometimes in other disciplines. The 'private' now becomes the 'public'; what was once implicit and unexpressed in professional practice now has to become explicit and explained to others.

The strategy

Here is a summary of the most important things teachers should take into account if they are to develop successful collaborative arrangements in co-teaching situations:

- Establish clear common goals for the collaboration.
- Define your respective roles and who is accountable for what, but accept joint responsibility for decisions and their outcomes.
- Take a problem-solving approach – with a sense that all those in the collaborative arrangement share ownership of the problem and its solution.
- Establish an atmosphere of trust and mutual respect for each other's expertise.
- Be willing to learn from others.
- Aim for consensus decision making.
- Agree on lesson objectives and structures, including teaching strategies and assessment methods.
- Agree on procedures for handling learners' disruptive or off-task behaviours.
- Ask for and give immediate and objective feedback to others in a non-threatening and non-judgemental manner.
- Give credit to others for their ideas and accomplishments.
- Develop procedures for resolving conflicts and manage these processes skilfully. Better still, anticipate possible conflicts and take steps to avoid them as far as possible. This is not to say that disagreements can, or even should be, avoided.
- Arrange periodic meetings to review progress in the collaborative arrangements.
- Seek support from the school's leadership for adequate, regular joint planning time.
- Clearly communicate with parents about any co-teaching arrangement.

See also **Strategies 29, 38** and **39**.

Source

What really works, Chapter 6. Op cit.

Strategy 41: Ensure successful transitions between education sectors

Rationale

Moving from one environment to another evokes different emotions among children: excitement, curiosity, trepidation, anxiety and even fear. All are faced with several moves during their educational careers: typically from home to early childhood education centre, to elementary/primary school, to high/secondary school, with some facing another transition to tertiary education. These transitions do not always proceed either smoothly or painlessly, especially for children who struggle academically or who experience social adjustment difficulties. Multiple factors influence each child's transition experience, with corresponding opportunities for educators – and parents/caregivers – to make it a successful and enjoyable one.

What is involved in making transitions between education sectors? At the most basic level, children have to adapt to new physical environments: buildings, the location of toilets, playgrounds, travelling to and from school, etc. But more significantly, they have to adapt to new groups of children and the challenge of forming new friendships. And, just as significantly, they have to adapt to new groups of educators who often take on different roles to those in their previous education environment. At home, too, parents/caregivers and extended family change their behaviours and expectations as their children face new demands.

The strategy

Preparing children for making transitions is very important. The best preparation is to ensure that they experience success and acceptance in their present environment before moving on to the next. More specific measures are also called for. These include the following:

- Ensure close collaboration between the 'sending' and the 'receiving' teachers by sharing information about the children making the transition and about the teaching strategies they experienced. It could also involve reciprocal visits by those involved to each other's institutions.
- Specifically prepare children for the transition by discussing what is involved, making orientation visits to the receiving environment and using videos to familiarize children with it.
- Involve parents/caregivers in the process by arranging orientation meetings with personnel from the receiving institutions, distributing information materials about the next steps and putting parents in touch with other parents (particularly appropriate for parents of children with special education needs and for different ethnic groups who may be unfamiliar with how the education system operates).
- Develop close collaboration among the various educational institutions in the local district (see **Strategy 29**).

See also **Strategy 18**.

Strategy 42: Ensure that classrooms have adequate physical environments

Rationale

Learners who spend time in well-designed, well-maintained classrooms that are comfortable, well lit, reasonably quiet and properly ventilated with healthy air, will learn more efficiently and enjoy their educational experiences. In such environments, teachers, too, will be healthier, happier and more effective as educators. There is ample evidence that improvements in classrooms' physical environments lead to improved academic performance and behaviours in children with special educational needs. These improvements should be guided by international standards set by such bodies as the World Health Organization.

The strategy

Physical space. Arrange learners' workspaces to facilitate flexible grouping and differentiated instruction by allowing for whole class, small-group and individual instruction. Some learners, for example those with autism, may need access to personal space, with calm, ordered, low-stimulus spaces, no confusing large spaces and safe indoor and outdoor places for withdrawal and to calm down. Classrooms (and schools) should be designed to enable ease of access for students with physical disabilities.

Temperature, humidity and ventilation. Several studies attest to the importance of attending to the air quality in classrooms. Research shows that by improving ventilation and air quality and setting optimal temperatures, students' attendance and achievement increases.

Lighting. Reviews of the effects of lighting in classrooms show that:

- the visual environment affects learners' ability to perceive visual stimuli and affects their mental attitudes and, therefore, their performance;
- day-lighting has the most positive effects on learners' achievement;
- since day-lighting as a sole source of lighting is not feasible, it should be supplemented by automatically controlled electric lighting that dims in response to daylight levels;
- lighting should be as glare-free and flicker-free as possible, especially when computers are being used.

Acoustics. Since much classroom learning takes place through listening and speaking, it is essential that students can hear educators' speech clearly. Unfortunately, this is not always the case, even with typical classrooms in many developed countries providing inadequate acoustical environments. This can have a major impact on students' opportunities to learn, especially for those with mild or fluctuating hearing loss, learning disabilities, attention disorders and language disabilities. One way of improving the acoustic environment is to introduce sound field amplification (a set up where a teacher has a small microphone and there are speakers distributed around the classroom), which has had encouraging results.

Sources

Diversities in education, Chapter 6. Op cit.
What really works, Chapter 21. Op cit.

Strategy 43: Identify and remediate learning and behavioural problems as early as possible at school

Rationale

Just as early intervention for infants and toddlers is important (see **Strategy** 7), so too is the early identification and remediation of children's lack of progress and behavioural difficulties at school. In a review, James Buckley (2009) concluded that 'a substantial body of research has shown that the early onset of behavioral and mental health problems during elementary school is associated with an increased risk for subsequent severe behavior and academic problems' (p. 195). He went on to note research that showed that 'in the absence of effective intervention, many students who exhibit serious behavior problems in the early elementary grades ... develop more significant antisocial and disruptive behavior patterns by the upper elementary or middle school grades' (ibid.). In a similar vein, the World Health Organization and World Bank (2011) emphasized that early identification and intervention can reduce the level of educational support children with disabilities may require throughout their schooling and ensure they reach their full potential.

While it is important that learning and behavioural difficulties be identified and intervention provided during the early childhood years, we must also recognize that in some children these difficulties only become apparent later during their time at school, sometimes only in adolescence. This is a time when children spend increasing amounts of time in more formal classrooms, with larger groups of peers and with the expectation they conform to certain standards of behaviour and demonstrate academic learning. Not all children adapt to this new environment. There should be procedures in place to identify who they are and, of course, provide appropriate remedial programmes when needed.

The strategy

Teachers should identify as early as possible any children showing learning and behavioural difficulties, by

- carrying out regular health checks, including screening for visual and hearing impairments;
- tracking children's academic progress against achievement standards;
- monitoring emotional and behavioural changes;
- being aware of some children becoming victims or perpetrators of bullying (including cyber bullying);
- regularly communicating with parents/caregivers regarding their children's behaviour and attitudes;
- following Response to Intervention guidelines (see **Strategy 44**); and
- seeking expert guidance.

Identification should always lead to remediation strategies, such as those recommended in this book.

Sources

Buckley, J.A. (2009). 'Introduction to this special issue: Implementing evidence-based interventions in elementary schools for students at risk for severe behavior disorders.' *Journal of Emotional and Behavioral Disorders, 17*(4), 195–196.

World Health Organization, & World Bank (2011). *World report on disability.* Geneva: World Health Organization.

Strategy 44: Employ Response to Intervention procedures

Rationale

Response to Intervention (RtI) is a tiered approach to the early identification of students at risk for learning disabilities or problem behaviour. It was originally developed as a means of determining whether students had a learning disability, as an alternative to an earlier approach based on the discrepancy between IQ and academic achievement.

In brief, RtI involves (a) tracking the progress of all students in a class; (b) identifying those whose levels and rates of performance are significantly below their peers; and (c) systematically assessing the impact of evidence-based teaching on their achievement. The RtI framework provides a system for delivering interventions of increasing intensity.

The strategy

RtI involves implementing three tiers of intervention. Each tier provides progressively more intense and individualized intervention, with the aim of preventing, reducing or eliminating serious and continuing learning difficulties or behavioural problems.

> *Tier I: core classroom instruction.* Sometimes referred to as 'primary prevention', this is the foundation of RtI. It contains the core curriculum, which should be effective for approximately 80–85% of students. It focuses on in-class support and group interventions for all students. The teaching programme should comprise evidence-based instruction and should be the responsibility of the general education teacher.

> *Tier II: supplemental instruction.* Sometimes referred to as 'secondary prevention', interventions are of moderate intensity. They serve approximately 15–20% of students who have been identified as having continuing difficulties and have not responded to normal instruction. Interventions at this level comprise targeted small group interventions for about an additional hour per week. This tier remains the responsibility of the general education teacher, but with the assistance of a relevant specialist.

> *Tier III: Instruction for intensive intervention.* Sometimes referred to as 'tertiary prevention', this tier serves approximately 5–10% (some say as few as 2%) of students with extreme difficulties in academic, social and/or behavioural domains who have not responded adequately to Tier I and Tier II efforts. Students receive intensive, individual and/or small group interventions, with daily monitoring of progress in critical skills. A trained specialist would be involved. If Tier III is not successful, a student is considered for the first time as potentially having a disability.

Note: students with severe or significant academic, social-emotional or behavioural problems (e.g. those with complex needs) would be 'triaged' directly into Tier III, rather than requiring them to first go through Tiers I and II.

See also **Strategy 38**.

Sources

Diversities in education, Chapter 6. Op cit.
What really works, Chapter 23. Op cit.

Strategy 45: Ensure that schools do not convey negative stereotypes that may stoke hostility against any religion

Rationale

Historically and contemporaneously, adherents to certain religions have suffered persecution and even death for their beliefs. Set up in 1948, the United Nations Special Rapporteur on Freedom of Religion or Belief has a brief 'to promote the adoption of measures at the national, regional and international levels to ensure the promotion and protection of the right to freedom of religion or belief'. In his 2014 report, the then Rapporteur noted that 'violence committed in the name of religion, that is, on the basis of or arrogated to religious tenets of the perpetrator, can lead to massive violations of human rights, including freedom of religion or belief'. He recommended 'concerted actions by all relevant stakeholders, including States, religious communities, interreligious dialogue initiatives, civil society organizations and media representatives, in order to contain and eventually eliminate the scourge of violence committed in the name of religion' (p. 1). Schools can and should do much in this regard, not only to eliminate religion-motivated violence, but also to promote religious tolerance.

The strategy

There are several steps educators can take to deal with religion-based violence and hostility at school. These include the following:

- The state should not support any schools that express contempt or hostility for any religion.
- Schools should promote a culture of respect, non-discrimination and appreciation of diversity within the larger society.
- Textbooks used in schools should not contain negative stereotypes and prejudices likely to stoke discrimination or hostile sentiments against any groups, including the followers of certain religions or holders of certain beliefs.
- Schools catering for refugee children should be particularly alert to any religious tensions carried over from their countries of origin.
- In schools where a range of religions is represented, the staff should closely monitor playground behaviour and social media to detect and deal with any signs of religious hostility or discrimination.

See also **Strategies 1, 24, 27, 28** and **47**.

Sources

Diversities in education, Chapter 5. Op cit.

United Nations. (2014). *Report of the Special Rapporteur on Freedom of Religion or Belief, Heiner Bielefeldt.* Geneva. URL: www.ohchr.org/EN/Issues/FreedomReligion/Pages/Annual.aspx

Strategy 46: Ensure that evolution is taught as part of the science curriculum, but that creationism is not

Rationale

One of the distinguishing features of the human species is our ability to deduce cause, agency and intent, attributes that helps us to survive across hugely diverse environments (see also **Chapter 8**). Sometimes in the past, these explanations were natural and eventually became established through science; at other times, they were supernatural and were incorporated into religion. In modern western society, religion's explanatory power has increasingly become usurped by science, with the origins of the universe being attributed to the Big Bang and evolutionary biology. Nevertheless, creationists still invoke God as a 'First Cause' who created the universe and every species, including humans.

So, should creationism or evolution – or both – be taught in schools? In 1968 the US Supreme Court took a position on this question when it considered the constitutionality of a 1928 Arkansas law forbidding the teaching of evolution in public schools. The Court found that this law was unconstitutional because it violated the separation of church and state. It made no finding as to the truth or otherwise of evolution. However, this issue did attract a comment from the UK Secretary of State for Education in 2014 when, in reply to a Parliamentary question, he said that:

> State-funded schools, including free schools and academies, should not teach creationism as an evidence-based scientific theory. Outside of science lessons, it is permissible for schools to cover creationism as part of religious education lessons, providing that this does not undermine the teaching of established scientific theory.

Consideration of the place of creationism in the school curricula must also include consideration of indoctrination. Indoctrination clearly takes place when (a) teaching an ideology as if it were the only possible one with any claim to rationality; and (b) teaching as though they are certain propositions the teacher knows to be uncertain and substantially disputed by other competent authorities.

The strategy

Quite simply, this strategy has two parts. First, the science curriculum should include the central role of evolution in the development of species and nothing should subtract from that during a learner's educational experiences. Second, since creationism is a central tenet of some religions, it is justifiable to include it in religious education programmes, provided it is not portrayed as a viable alternative to evolution.

See also **Strategy 48**.

Source

Diversities in education, Chapter 5. Op cit.

Strategy 47: Ensure that students are taught about their rights and responsibilities under international human rights conventions and their own country's human rights legislation

Rationale

In **Strategy 1**, I focused on governments' responsibilities to recognize the rights and freedoms specified in relevant international conventions generated by the *Universal Declaration of Human Rights* (UDHR). As specified in Article 7 of the UDHR,

> All are equal before the law and are entitled without any discrimination to equal protection of the law. All are entitled to equal protection against any discrimination in violation of this Declaration and against any incitement to such discrimination.

I turn now to the role of schools in recognizing and implementing these rights. Schools are, of course, an essential tool for meeting the State's international obligations to recognize, protect, promote and fulfill human rights, particularly of the most disadvantaged children. They do this by respecting rights to dignity, identity, safety, fair treatment, expression and participation. As well, schools should be delivering programmes for teaching learners about human rights. These are commonly referred to as Human Rights Education (HRE). According to UNESCO, HRE is an integral part of the right to education and is increasingly gaining recognition as a human right in itself. Knowledge of rights and freedoms is considered a fundamental tool to guarantee respect for the rights of all.

According to UNESCO, education should encompass values such as peace, non-discrimination, equality, justice, non-violence, tolerance and respect for human dignity. To achieve these criteria, HRE means implementing rights throughout the whole education system and in all learning environments.

In the English county of Hampshire within the United Kingdom, the approach has been credited with producing the following results in primary and secondary schools: a decline in bullying; less adversarial children's approaches to resolving conflict; and improved school attendance.

The strategy

- HRE should be recognized as being an essential tool for meeting the State's international obligation to recognize, protect, promote and fulfill human rights.
- There should be coordinated strategic approach to designing and implementing HRE.
- HRE should be designed in collaboration with government and non-government agencies and organizations such as UNESCO.
- HRE should be directed at ensuring that students learn to respect, protect and fulfil the rights of others.

For an example of a detailed HRE programme, see Duvivier (2009).

Sources

Diversities in education, Chapter 1. Op cit.
Duvivier, A. (2009). *Compasito human rights education handbook*. Council of Europe.

Strategy 48: Develop critical thinking skills

Rationale

We are living in an era of social media generating 'fake news' and facilitating cyber bullying, an era when too many politicians seek to gain power by playing on prejudice and misinformation, an era when ethnic, religious and gender minorities are exposed to discrimination and even violence, an era when some children continue to be indoctrinated into beliefs which confound evidence, an era when democratic values and the rights of minorities are increasingly under threat…

I believe that at least some of these trends can be attributed to deficits in critical thinking in our populations. I further assert that educators must assume some responsibility for these deficits and take active steps to rectify them.

So, what is critical thinking? A good starting point is philosopher John Dewey's 1933 concept of 'reflexive thinking', which he defined as 'an active, persistent, and careful consideration of a belief or a supposed form of knowledge in the light of the grounds which support it and the further conclusions which it tends' (Dewey, 1991, p. 6). Typically, critical thinking is believed to include the component skills of analyzing arguments, making inferences by using inductive or deductive reasoning, judging or evaluating and making decisions or solving problems (Lai, 2011).

The strategy

Of particular relevance to the theme of this book, educators should, without fear or favour, critically analyze such issues as racism, sexism, economic inequalities, disabilism, religion, politics, culture, indoctrination, press freedom and social media.

This requires that propositions should be examined from all angles and students taught the skills of textual and media analysis. Above all, they should be encouraged to seek and discuss evidence and to question and challenge assumptions.

Most, if not all, of the issues I nominate should be studied from an historical perspective.

Teachers also need to be critical thinkers, with a drive to critically examine the systems in which they operate as well as their professional practices. In turn, these requirements have implications for the nature of initial and ongoing teacher education.

Several other strategies presented in this book also bear on critical thinking, most notably **Strategies 27**, **46**, **57** and **76**.

Sources

Dewey, J. (1991). *How we think*. Buffalo, NY. Prometheus Books.

Gormley, W.T. (2017). *The critical advantage: Developing critical thinking skills in school*. Harvard Education Press.

Lai, E. (2011). *Critical thinking: A literature review*. Research report. Pearson.

6

CLASSROOMS

Innovative learning environments

The nature of learning spaces we have traditionally referred to as 'classrooms' is undergoing profound change in many countries. You will be familiar with the traditional idea of a classroom comprising a single teacher conveying knowledge to a group of same-age children sitting at individual desks arranged in rows in a classroom bounded by four walls, with the teacher directing all pupils' in a simultaneous study of the same section of the curriculum, with minimal access to technology. This approach is being replaced by what is variously termed the 'modern learning environment' or the 'innovative learning environment' (ILE), which has three main characteristics:

1   *Flexibility:* the ability to combine two–three classes into one for team-teaching, with classes able to be split into small groups. Different classes can be combined to study complementary learning areas. Flexibility not only applies to the architecture, but also to the furniture, enabling various groupings and to take account of students' visuo-spatial (place and space) learning preferences.
2   *Openness:* an ILE school has fewer walls and usually no corridors or hallways. It has a learning common (or hub) which is a central teaching and learning space that can be shared by several classes with break-out spaces for small groups or individual study. Since several teachers and teacher assistants share the learning common, there are opportunities to observe and learn from the teaching of others and be observed in return.
3   *Access to resources:* a learning common and its breakout space allow for a range of different activities, such as reading, group work, project space, wet areas and reflection. As well, a mixture of wireless and wired technology offers access as and when students need it.

While there is good evidence for components of ILE having a positive effect on student learning, Harry Daniels (2017) has recently pointed out that 'the empirical research base is very limited regarding the importance of the visuo-spatial (place and space) in learning and teaching, and in the general creation of a suitable educational environment'. Daniels and his colleagues are currently investigating this issue.

However a classroom or an ILE is defined, the 23 pedagogical strategies I list in this chapter are all applicable and should be used when the circumstances warrant them.

Sources

Daniels, H. (2017). *Design matters? The effects of new schools on students', teachers' and parents' actions and perceptions.* URL: www.education.ox.ac.uk/about-us/design-matters-website-launched/

Strategy 49: Recognize and adjust to the diverse worldviews of different groups of learners

Rationale

A truism of teaching is that one should start from what students already know and build out from that. This is no less true for starting with an understanding of their worldviews – the frameworks of ideas and attitudes about the world and themselves – that they bring to school. These may be at variance with those held by some or many of their peers and their teachers. It is thus a challenge to educators to understand the parameters of these worldviews and to determine how they should be taken into account in their teaching and in their relationships with parents. In doing so, it must be noted that any particular ethnic, religious or social group will have a diversity of worldviews and should not be stereotyped; some will hold them firmly, others not at all, and still others with a low level of commitment.

Normally associated with religion, social class and ethnicity, there is now a recognition that different disabilities also have distinctive worldviews. It has long been argued that deaf people share a worldview experienced primarily through visual rather than auditory experiences. Also, rather than seeing autistic behaviours as signs of pathology, Barry Prizant (2015) considers them as part of a range of strategies to cope with a world that feels chaotic and overwhelming.

The strategy

It is important that educators take account of the different worldviews of students and their families. This can be done by adopting strategies such as the following:

- recognize that all students have worldviews composed of social, familial, religious, linguistic and ethnically related practices that shape the ways in which they see the world and interact with it;
- sensitize students to the idea that humans have developed a range of different worldviews, and that this breadth of human life enriches all of us;
- incorporate an appreciation of different expressions of creativity, including artefacts, symbols, texts, objects, dress and food into learning about one another;
- become familiar with children's different sense-making worldviews and determine how far it is morally justified to support them or to challenge them; and
- recognize that as well as worldviews derived from their group membership, individuals have their own worldviews. See also **Chapter 8**.

See also **Strategy 50**.

Sources

Diversities in education, Chapters 3, 4 and 5. Op cit.
Prizant, B. (2015). *Uniquely human: A different way of seeing autism.* Simon & Schuster.

Strategy 50: Recognize and adjust to the diverse cultural and social capital of different groups of learners

Rationale

As I pointed out in **Strategy 49**, many children who come from certain class, gender, cultural, religious and disability backgrounds have distinctive worldviews. Two major contributors to these worldviews are cultural and social capital.

> *Cultural capital.* This comprises tangible and intangible assets, such as education and specialized knowledge and skills that confer social status and power within a society. It is reflected in language and communication skills, the availability of books and the Internet, parents' aspirations for their children, their involvement in school activities and knowledge of how to make their way around the education system. According to Bourdieu and Passeron (1977), children who inherit the cultural capital of the education system begin their schooling with an advantage they are likely to maintain.

> *Social capital.* Robert Putnam (2015) has defined this as comprising different kinds of connectedness, such as informal links to relatives, friends and acquaintances, as well as participation in communal functions such as churches, sports and volunteer activities. Putnam is particularly concerned at the differences in social capital among America's classes, pointing to the growing gulf between how the rich and the poor raise their children. For example, he observed that educated parents engage in Socratic dialogue with their children, helping them to make up their own minds about right and wrong, true and false.

The strategy

The key point to recognize is that many children come to school with cultural and social capital that differs from the prevailing norms and expectations of schools.

The challenge to educators is to determine how far they can and should go in accommodating the cultural and social capital of diverse groups. At stake here is the comfort, even the feelings of safety that children will experience in the school environments that they are (usually) compelled to attend. In turn, this will impact on their self-esteem, identities, sense of empowerment and, ultimately, their behaviour and achievement.

However, I also believe that one of the functions of education is to broaden learners' choices and to increase their cultural and social capital and to do this sensitively and with respect to their backgrounds.

Sources

Bourdieu, P., & Passeron, J.C. (1977). *Reproduction in education, society and culture.* London: Sage.
Diversities in education, Chapters 1 and 3. Op cit.
Putnam, R.D. (2015). *Our kids: The American dream in crisis.* New York: Simon & Schuster.

Strategy 51: Employ formative assessment

Rationale

Assessment is increasingly being seen as serving educational purposes by promoting learning and by guiding teaching. It should provide the best possible account of what a learner knows, can do, or has experienced.

There are two basic types of assessment: summative and formative. Briefly, *summative* assessment is concerned with evaluating learners' performances at the end of a module or a course. The results count towards making a final judgement on what the learners have achieved. It is usually high stakes. *Formative* assessment evaluates learners' progress during a course or module so that they have opportunities to improve. It is as much assessment *for* learning as assessment *of* learning.

Simply being exposed to information or concepts does not guarantee that students will learn them. Rather, it is helpful if teachers frequently probe for knowledge in a variety of ways and at different times to ensure that learners understand, retain and generalize new concepts. This information gives teachers a better idea of their learners' needs and enables them to fine-tune their teaching. It also enables them to give appropriate feedback to their students (see **Strategy 65**).

The strategy

Teachers should use formative assessment to diagnose why some learners are not succeeding and to adapt the curriculum and re-design their teaching to rectify any problems. For example, it may be necessary to re-teach a concept, change the pace of a unit, clarify the content or review material with which the students experience difficulty.

There are three things to consider when planning the use of formative assessment:

1   *Deciding what information is needed.* This requires that teachers know their students, how they best learn and what objectives they have for them. Formative assessment should provide descriptions of what has or has not been understood.
2   *Determining when the information is needed.* This may be before a lesson or unit, when students are pre-tested to determine what they already know about the topic. Or it may be during the teaching of it, when the focus is on the interactions between the teacher and the students or on the interactions among the students.
3   *Selecting the means for collecting information.* This typically includes a range of approaches for assessing students' knowledge and skills, some formal and others informal. These may include checklists, quizzes, classroom tests, portfolios, observations, learning journals, assignments, observations and conferences/interviews with individuals or small groups.

Source

What really works, Chapter 17. Op cit.

Strategy 52: Implement Universal Design for Learning

Rationale

Universal Design for Learning (UDL) is a multi-component strategy for guiding educational practice that provides flexibility in the ways information is presented, in the ways students respond or demonstrate knowledge and skills, and in the ways they are engaged. It is intended to reduce barriers in instruction, provide appropriate accommodations, supports and challenges, and maintain high achievement expectations for all students. It applies to all facets of education: from curriculum, assessment and pedagogy to classroom and school design. It challenges teachers to design and implement instruction in a flexible manner that meets the needs of diverse learners, thus increasing their engagement.

In a word, UDL requires *differentiation*, a theme I take up later in **Strategy 75**.

A recent meta-analysis supported claims regarding the effectiveness of UDL in improving the learning processes for all students (Capp, 2017). However, the limited availability of empirical evidence involving pre- and post-tests was also noted. The author therefore recommended that future research should be carried out to further examine the impact of UDL on the learning process, as well as on its educational outcomes.

The strategy

UDL is based on three principles:

1 multiple ways of representing knowledge during the learning process, e.g.

- use multiple examples and diverse materials, including multimedia;
- provide the same information through different modalities (vision, hearing, touch);
- provide information in adjustable formats (e.g. text and graphics that can be enlarged, sounds that can be amplified, text equivalents for spoken language and spoken descriptions of images and graphics).

2 multiple ways of action and expression, e.g.

- provide students with choice in terms of both how they access information and how they represent their knowledge and understanding;
- provide options for physical action through appropriate assistive technology such as switches, expanded keyboards etc. (see **Strategy 66**);
- provide options for expression and communication (e.g. compose in text, speech, drawing, film, music, dance, visual art video, etc.).

3 multiple means of engagement, e.g.

- provide options for stimulating interest and engaging learners, for example by providing choices;
- maximize relevance and authenticity of lesson content;
- minimize threats and distractions; and
- encourage effort and persistence.

Sources

Capp, M.J. (2017). 'The effectiveness of universal design for learning: A meta-analysis of literature between 2013 and 2016.' *International Journal of Inclusive Education, 21*(8), 1–17.
Diversities in education, Chapter 1. Op cit.
What really works, Chapter 22. Op cit.

Strategy 53: Set high, but realistic, standards

Rationale

Many of the children who are the subject of this book have, through prolonged failure, rejected the notion that they are capable of learning. They can be at further risk if their educators and parents have similarly low expectations for their performances.

The power of teacher expectancy was dramatically illustrated in a classic study by Rosenthal and Jacobsen (1968). They conducted an experiment with first and second grade students in a public elementary school, telling teachers that certain children could be expected to be 'growth spurters', based on the students' results on a non-existent test. In point of fact, the children designated as 'spurters' were chosen at random. Rosenthal and Jacobsen found that teachers' high expectations led to subsequent high levels of IQ test performance in these children.

In the United Kingdom, an Ofsted analysis of a sample of inspection reports for out-standing schools in areas of economic deprivation identified as a critical factor for success staff being ambitious in their expectations of students' achievement.

I suspect that one of the reasons teachers may have low expectations for children from low-SES or ethnic minority homes has to do with their perceptions of the cultural and social capital these children bring to school (see **Strategy 50**).

It may well be, too, that parents' high expectations contribute significantly to Asian children, such as those with Chinese and Indian backgrounds, out-performing other ethnic minorities in many western countries.

The strategy

Teachers should:

- believe all students can learn and convey to them that they have the ability to master essential learning outcomes;
- constantly strive to raise the expectations of learners and their parents;
- help learners accept that achievement results from effort, as much as from ability;
- help learners develop strong beliefs in their own ability: as Henry Ford once stated, 'Whether you think you can or you can't, you're right'; and
- set clear and consistent expectations for student behaviour in class and in the larger school setting.

A word of caution to conclude: note that this strategy includes the word 'realistic'. It is as dangerous to set standards too high as to set standards too low.

Sources

Diversities in education, Chapters 3 and 4. Op cit.

Ofsted (2007). *The Annual Report of Her Majesty's Chief Inspector of Education, Children's Services and Skills 2006/07*. London.

Rosenthal, R., & Jacobson, L. (1968). *Pygmalion in the classroom*. New York: Holt, Rinehart & Winston.

What really works, Chapter 24. Op cit.

Strategy 54: Employ cooperative group teaching

Rationale

Cooperative group teaching is based on two main ideas about learning. First, it recognizes that when learners cooperate, or collaborate, it has a synergistic effect. In other words, by working together learners can often achieve a result greater than the sum of their individual efforts or capabilities. Second, it recognizes that much of our knowledge is socially constructed; that is, we learn from others in our immediate environments – our families, our friendship groups and our workplaces. Thus, cooperative group teaching is a 'natural' way of teaching and learning. Furthermore, it can influence the ethos of a class and school by developing the values of helping and caring. Ultimately, it can contribute to making a classroom more cohesive and respectful of diversity.

The strategy

There are two aspects to this strategy: (1) mutual assistance group work, and (2) jig-saw group work. The first involves more able members of a group providing support or assistance to less able members. The second involves all members of a group contributing to achieve a group goal, with all learners having something unique to offer.

In deciding on the composition of groups, a choice has to be made between ability grouping and mixed ability grouping. My preference is for a combination of both types, but with mixed ability groups on most occasions. If ability grouping is used too much, it runs the risk of negating inclusive education.

To bring about successful cooperative group learning, teachers should attend to these main issues:

- Use cooperative learning mainly after learners have acquired sufficient knowledge to be involved in discussion and learning with their peers.
- Design activities suitable for all members of the group.
- In the case of mutual assistance groups, members should be instructed as to how they should provide assistance.
- In the case of jig-saw activities, activities should be within the competence of all members of the group.
- Teach group process skills such as listening, making eye contact, communicating clearly, asking questions, providing leadership, building trust, making decisions, managing conflict, giving encouragement, recognizing contributions, understanding other learners' points of view and (importantly) respecting individual differences.
- Take care in allocating learners to groups to ensure they are compatible.
- Carefully monitor the functioning and outputs of the groups.

Source

What really works, Chapter 3. Op cit.

Strategy 55: Employ peer tutoring

Rationale

Peers play multiple roles in supporting and teaching each other – a 'natural' social relationship that you should be capitalize on (see also **Strategy 54**). Peer tutoring is based on the idea that children learn a great deal from each other. It often occurs spontaneously in schools, neighbourhoods and in homes.

Peer tutoring is a powerful tool for increasing the overall effectiveness of teaching in inclusive classrooms. It can be used across subject areas.

Properly handled, peer tutoring brings benefits to:

- *tutees*, by being provided with increased individual attention, work pitched at their instructional level, repeated practice, immediate feedback, peer support and additional time engaged with tasks;
- *tutors*, who can make gains by having their own skills reinforced and expanded, as well as by having their self confidence and sensitivity to others enhanced; and
- *educators*, by enabling them to increase the level of cooperation in their classes and giving them more time to spend with other learners.

The strategy

Quite simply, peer tutoring involves one learner (the 'tutor') providing a learning experience for another learner (the 'tutee'), under a teacher's supervision. It is best used to promote fluency through practising or reviewing skills or knowledge, rather than as a means of initially teaching skills or knowledge.

Peer tutoring can take many forms, with pairs comprising different combinations according to age and ability level. A common pattern is for a more able learner to tutor a less able learner of the same age. A variant involves an older learner tutoring a younger learner.

To be successful, peer tutoring has to be carefully planned and sensitively supervised. In a reading session, for example:

- Use a structured lesson format, with clear goals and a systematic step-by-step approach.
- Carefully select reading material to ensure it is within the tutee's level of understanding.
- Train the tutors in approaches to presenting the material. A useful method is *Pause, Prompt, Praise*, used when a learner is reading aloud with a partner. Thus, *Pause*: when the learner makes an error, wait for at least 5 seconds for him or her to self-correct; *Prompt*: if the learner still does not know the word, give some hints before saying the word; *Praise*: give praise for attempts at saying the word.
- Set up tutoring sessions for a limited time period. For example: 10-minute sessions, 3 times per week for 2 weeks.
- Actively supervise the tutoring.

Source

What really works, Chapter 4. Op cit.

Strategy 56: Develop social skills training

Rationale

Most children quite readily acquire the social skills appropriate to their culture, but some do not and must be explicitly taught them. Some have poor social perception and consequently lack social skills. This is particularly true of those with autism and emotional, behavioural disorders and severe disabilities. And, of course, different cultural groups may vary in the ways they relate to others.

While social skills are important at all ages, they are particularly important during adolescence, when inadequate social skills can lead to low social status among peers and a range of negative outcomes, including poor achievement, dropout, victimization and even violence.

The strategy

Social skills training (SST) involves helping learners establish and maintain positive interactions with others, focusing on:

- *Social sensitivity*: accurately making sense of the meaning of a social event.
- *Role-taking*: 'reading' people and understanding how they are experiencing the world.
- *Social comprehension*: understanding friendships and social reciprocity.
- *Social communication*: understanding how to intervene effectively and influence the behaviour of others.
- *Social problem-solving*: resolving conflicts and understanding how to influence the behaviour of others to achieve desired goals.

It is unrealistic to expect that SST will always lead to close friendships. Such relationships are based on a whole host of other factors, including mutual interests, compatibility, contacts in the neighbourhood, family connections and so on.

The skills most widely associated with social competence include:

- *conversation skills*: greetings, saying 'please' or 'thank you', learning and using names, selecting appropriate topics, keeping conversations alive, making and maintaining eye contact (but note cultural differences here), employing appropriate facial expressions, using an appropriate tone of voice, standing in appropriate positions relative to others, inhibiting impulsive behaviour and active listening;
- *coping with conflict*: saying 'No', dealing with aggressive persons, responding to teasing, apologizing, gaining attention, asking for help, dealing with criticism, negotiating, persuading, responding to others' needs, respecting individual differences; and
- *friendship skills*: making friends, giving and accepting thanks, initiating and responding to humour, taking turns, and being in tune with the peer group culture (e.g. knowing about fashion, music, films, tv...).

A range of methods can be employed to teach social skills, including describing and discussing these skills and their importance, role playing, miming, analysis of video clips, literature analysis, reinforcing appropriate behaviours, prompting and explicit feedback.

See also **Strategy 57**.

Source

What really works, Chapter 5. Op cit.

Strategy 57: Enhance students' social and emotional learning

Rationale

Mental health problems and associated behaviours in students are concerning educators around the world. These include aggressiveness, bullying, depression, anxiety and suicide. Such problems are increasingly being ascribed to children's inadequate social and emotional learning (SEL).

The cornerstone of educational programmes directed at enhancing children's social and emotional learning is the delivery of five essential skills and competencies to students (CASEL, 2015).

Self-awareness: The ability to accurately recognize one's own emotions and thoughts and their influence on behaviour. This includes accurately assessing one's strengths and limitations and possessing a well-grounded sense of confidence and optimism.

Self-management: The ability to regulate one's emotions, thoughts and behaviours effectively in different situations. This includes managing stress, controlling impulses, motivating oneself and setting and working towards achieving personal and academic goals.

Social awareness: The ability to take the perspective of and empathize with others from diverse backgrounds and cultures, to understand social and ethical norms for behaviour and to recognize family, school and community resources and supports.

Relationship skills: The ability to establish and maintain healthy and rewarding relationships with diverse individuals and groups. This includes communicating clearly, listening actively, cooperating, resisting inappropriate social pressure, negotiating conflict constructively and seeking and offering help when needed.

Responsible decision-making: The ability to make constructive and respectful choices about personal behaviour and social interactions based on consideration of ethical standards, safety concerns, social norms, the realistic evaluation of consequences of various actions and the well-being of oneself and others.

The strategy

There is a substantial and growing evidence base showing the effectiveness of SEL programmes in reducing emotional distress, improving the behaviours and enhancing the academic achievement of children. Schools with concerns about SEL should select from the growing range of evidence-based programmes and implement them with fidelity.

SEL programmes can be delivered through a mix of stand-alone lessons and integration into regular subject lessons. These are more powerful when reinforced in all the contexts that affect children's learning and development.

Ideally, parents/caregivers should be involved in the delivery of SEL programmes. At a minimum, they should be informed about the aims and approaches being implemented by the school.

In analyzing children's SEL difficulties, use should be made of the social information processing model as outlined by Ogden and Hagen (2014).

See also **Strategies 56** and **76**.

Sources

Collaborative for Academic, Social, and Emotional Learning (CASEL) (2015). *Effective social and emotional learning programs. Middle and high school edition.* Chicago.

Ogden, T., & Hagen, K.A. (2014). *Adolescent mental health: Prevention and intervention.* Routledge.

Strategy 58: Employ cognitive strategy instruction

Rationale

Cognitive development involves the construction of thought processes, including remembering, reasoning, problem solving and information processing, and the application of these abilities to achieve major developmental tasks. Such development varies from individual to individual and competence spans a range from giftedness to intellectual disabilities, including autistic spectrum disorder, dyslexia and ADHD.

Most learners develop efficient and effective cognitive skills through their life experiences, with minimal teaching of how to go about the process. Others, however, don't appear to use appropriate techniques to help them learn. They either don't know what strategies to use, or use the wrong ones, or don't spontaneously use strategies at all. These deficiencies may compound other disabilities or they may constitute the disability itself.

Cognitive strategy instruction (CSI) focuses on ways of assisting learners to acquire cognitive strategies. It does this by helping them to (a) organize information so that its complexity is reduced, and/or (b) integrate information into their existing knowledge. It involves teaching learners methods for accomplishing various kinds of tasks. It includes teaching skills such as visualization, planning, self-regulation, memorizing, analyzing, predicting, making associations, using cues and thinking about thinking (i.e. metacognition). In a nutshell, with CSI, teachers are as much concerned with teaching their students *how to learn* as teaching them the subject matter of the curriculum.

The strategy

Here are some examples of effective CSI for teachers:

- Devote instructional time to the processes, as well as the products of learning.
- Model effective strategies by thinking aloud while you are working on problems.
- Give learners practice in using a strategy immediately after it has been modelled.
- Analyze tasks in terms of the cognitive strategies involved.
- Embed CSI in all your teaching.
- Give guided practice in the use of strategies.
- Help learners become aware of learning processes and strategies.
- Encourage learners to self evaluate the quality of their completed work, their understanding of an area of work, or their effort in relation to task demands.
- Increase metacognitive awareness.
- Teach generic cognitive strategies that apply across subjects, e.g. *think ahead, think during* and *think back* when solving a problem.
- Teach subject-specific cognitive strategies, e.g. writing stories, solving mathematical problems.

See also **Strategies 59, 61** and **76**.

Sources

Diversities in education, Chapter 1. Op cit.
What really works, Chapter 8. Op cit.

Strategy 59: Employ memory strategies instruction

Rationale

Benjamin Bloom (1987) argued that learners will retain 10% of what they read, 20% of what they hear, 30% of what they see, 50% of what they see and hear, 70% of what they say and 90% of what they say and do.

Memory is by far the most important capacity possessed by humans and must be nurtured in all learners. Some may have difficulty in remembering and will need help.

There are three main types of memory:

Primary memory. Some elements of a task will automatically elicit associations with past experiences. Examples of primary memory include multiplication tables, and the alphabet.

Short-term memory. Some elements of a task and the information necessary to solve a problem will be held in a short-term memory store. Sometimes referred to as our 'working memory', its job is to temporarily store small amounts of information while it is being used.

Long-term memory. For tasks of moderate to high complexity, learners have to 'search' their long- term memory store to retrieve relevant information. This memory is some-times referred to as the 'permanent memory' and is characterized by enduring changes in the network of neural connections among the various bits of information stored there (see **Strategy 31**).

The strategy

Classroom practices to enhance memory include:

- Recognize that learners must be motivated to want to learn if they are to remember things.
- Provide learners with ample repetition and drills to build up a primary memory store. This does not mean using drill and rote learning for all classroom learning; it plays a role, but must not be over-done.
- Employ mnemonics strategies.
- Ensure that learners attend to critical features of tasks and ignore the 'noise' that might surround them. One of the key ways of doing this is by means of novelty.
- Recognize that how we feel about something can be just as important in determining what we remember as what we think about it.
- Present information in such a way that learners have time to process it.
- Transform material into visual representations of knowledge, concepts or ideas.
- Above all, learners should understand what it is they are expected to remember.

See also **Strategy 60**.

Sources

Bloom, B. (1987). *The closing of the American mind*. New York: Simon & Schuster.
What really works, Chapters 2 and 10. Op cit.

Strategy 60: Employ review and practice

Rationale

'Practice makes perfect' is a saying with a sound evidential basis. It is rare that 'one-shot' learning takes place. For the most part, we need repeated opportunities to learn a concept or a skill; for much of our learning we require repeated experiences of a skill or a concept for it to become readily available in our memory.

The purpose of the strategy is to help learners to 'internalize' concepts and skills once they have been initially taught. All learners benefit from this strategy, but those with significant cognitive needs require more opportunities to practice new material and to review previously taught material.

This strategy builds on the extensive and convincing literature on the psychological concept of *mass practice*, as distinct from *spaced practice*. The former involves several repetitions at one time, the latter several repetitions distributed over a period of time. Research supports both being used, but strongly favours spaced practice. In Hattie's (2009) synthesis of two meta-analyses involving spaced and massed practice, he found an effect size of 0.71 in favour of the former.

Another underlying point is that the act of retrieving information from the memory on several occasions acts as a 'memory modifier'. This means that retrieved information, rather than being left in the same state, becomes more retrievable in the future than it would have been had it not been accessed.

The strategy

Educators can enhance learning by ensuring they:

- Provide learners with adequate opportunities to engage with the same idea on *different occasions*. As a rule of thumb, learners need at least four different occasions when they engage with a concept if they are to remember it. This can be reduced to three for older and more able learners but should be increased to five or more for less able learners. Whatever the number of rehearsals or reviews, each of them should be separated by no more than a two-day interval.
- Provide learners with adequate opportunities to practice new skills in *different contexts* classrooms, playgrounds, homes, communities and so on.
- Review previously learned concepts, providing feedback and re-teaching if necessary, at the beginning of new lessons in the same area.
- Regularly carry out within-class reviews by frequently asking questions: some calling for specific answers, others for explanations of the answers (see also **Strategy 51**).
- Provide out-of-class practice, including homework.
- Provide computer-assisted practice.

See also **Strategy 59**.

Sources

Hattie, J. (2009). *Visible learning*. Routledge.
What really works, Chapter 11. Op cit.

Strategy 61: Employ reciprocal teaching

Rationale

Reciprocal teaching (RT) involves teaching learners, by means of guided practice, how to improve their reading comprehension. It shows them how to predict, clarify, question and summarize what is in a text. It typically involves an educator being very active initially, assisting learners to use strategies for comprehending written material and then gradually reducing support as learners become more skilled.

RT is mainly intended to improve the comprehension skills of learners who can decode texts, but have difficulty in comprehending them. It is a method for teaching comprehension, not word recognition skills.

RT is based on the Vygotskian principle that cognitive development is strongly influenced by interacting with more knowledgeable people (experts, educators, parents and more skilled peers). These interactions lead to strategies becoming internalized and made one's own. According to Vygotsky (1978), the *zone of proximal development* is the area between the actual development of a learner and his or her level of potential development, and is the area where instruction should take place.

A comprehensive review of 16 quantitative RT studies, including six with below-average learners, found a median effect size of 0.88 when experimenter-developed comprehension tests were used. The effect size was somewhat lower (0.32) when standardized tests were used. This analysis also showed that RT was most effective for older and poorer reading students (Rosenshine & Meister, 1994).

The strategy

RT takes place within a dialogue between an educator and learners while segments of text are studied. The following sequence typically takes place:

- Ask learners to read a passage of text silently, or else the teacher reads it orally.
- Begin the discussion by asking questions about the content of the passage, and give learners an opportunity to raise additional questions.
- Move on to work out the gist of the passage and summarize it.
- Clarify words or phrases that are unclear, unfamiliar or ambiguous.
- Finally, ask for predictions regarding what might occur next in the text. Learners may base these on their prior knowledge of the topic, clues provided in the passage or issues they hope the author will address in the remainder of the text.

See also **Strategy 58**.

Sources

Rosenshine, B. & Meister, C. (1994). 'Reciprocal teaching: A review of the research.' *Review of Educational Research, 64*(4), 479–530.

Vygotsky, L.S. (1978). *Mind in society: The development of higher psychological processes.* Cambridge, MA: Harvard University Press.

What really works, Chapter 12. Op cit.

Strategy 62: Employ behavioural approaches

Rationale

It has long been known that human beings (and other animals) will repeat actions that bring them satisfaction and discontinue those that don't. Behavioural approaches build on this simple principle, but go beyond it. The essence of this strategy is summarized in the acrostic, A-B-C (Antecedent-Behaviour-Consequence). This mean that events which occur either before or after learners engage in a verbal or physical act affect their subsequent behaviour. Antecedents are environmental events that cue or trigger behaviour. Consequences are environmental events that follow behaviour and influence the probability of that behaviour recurring in the future.

The strategy

This strategy involves a teacher selecting from various combinations of the following behaviours:

Controlling antecedents. In setting up tasks, teachers have several options from which to choose. They can:

- control the level of task difficulty by setting tasks which are neither too hard nor too easy;
- provide advance organizers (for example, ask learners to see what the headings might indicate about the material to be read);
- use verbal, gestural and physical prompts or graphic organizers to supplement general instructions;
- provide suitable, stimulating materials; and
- use picture schedules to remind learners about the steps to be followed (especially useful with autistic learners).

Controlling consequences. When a learner does something, teachers have several options. They can respond by:

- adding something pleasant; i.e. *positive reinforcement;*
- adding something unpleasant; i.e. *punishment type I;*
- removing something pleasant; i.e. *punishment type II;*
- removing something unpleasant; i.e. *negative reinforcement;*
- withholding any positive reinforcement for any behaviour; i.e. *extinction.*

Of these options, positive reinforcement is by far the most successful strategy. It is very important to select reinforcers that are important, significant or meaningful to learners at a particular time and place. As a rule of thumb, *continuous positive reinforcement* (i.e. given on as many occasions as practicable) should be given while a learner is learning a particular behaviour. Once that behaviour is established and maintenance is the objective, then *intermittent positive reinforcement* (i.e., reinforcing occasional correct responses) is all that is required.

There are other varieties of reinforcement that can be very useful in school settings. One is *differential reinforcement of incompatible behaviour,* when a reward is presented after a learner performs a behaviour incompatible with the undesired behaviour. For example, a boy who frequently engages in self-injurious behaviour may be reinforced for playing with toys with his hands for a predetermined period of time.

Source

What really works, Chapter 13. Op cit.

Strategy 63: Employ cognitive behavioural therapy

Rationale

Cognitive Behavioural Therapy (CBT) centres on changing a person's negative thinking patterns, which in turn leads to changes in behaviour and, ultimately, to a reduction or elimination of feelings of anxiety or depression. It is based on the assumption that our thinking (hence *cognitive*) causes us to feel and act (hence *behavioural*) the way we do. The goal is to help individuals unlearn their unwanted reactions and to learn new ways of reacting to situations.

Originally developed for adults with depression or anxiety conditions, CBT has successfully been extended to children and adolescents. It has not only been used to treat depression and anxiety disorders, but also aggressiveness, school refusal and post-traumatic stress disorders resulting from such events as sexual and physical abuse, divorce in the family, violence and natural disasters.

While this strategy is probably of greater relevance to psychiatrists, psychologists and counsellors, I believe classroom educators should also understand its fundamental principles (a) because they can be applied to some of their teaching and (b) because they would need to work closely with any professionals who are employing CBT with learners in their classes.

The strategy

Many of the features of CBT could guide educators' practices. Every day teachers work with learners who may not feel good about themselves as a result of difficulties they experience with the curriculum or in relating to their peers or in their home lives. Teachers' should therefore (a) anticipate such difficulties and take steps to avoid them, and (b) equip learners with skills to deal with difficulties when they occur by helping them to 'think' their way through them.

One approach is 'The ABC Technique of Irrational Beliefs', which involves dealing with:

A: the activating event: the situation that leads to negative thinking (e.g. failing a mathematics test);
B: the belief: the negative thoughts that occur (e.g. 'If I cannot do math, I am useless'); and
C: the consequence: the negative feelings and dysfunctional behaviours (e.g. 'I really am useless – in fact, I am worthless', and the person is therefore at risk for depression, anger and anxiety).

Following such an analysis, the therapist works with the person to 're-frame' the problem. This involves challenging negative thoughts to re-interpret them in a more realistic light, leading, one expects, to more rational beliefs and more appropriate behaviours.

Source

What really works, Chapter 15. Op cit.

Strategy 64: Employ Direct Instruction

Rationale

Direct Instruction (DI) centres on teacher-directed, explicit, systematic teaching based on scripted lesson plans and frequent assessment. Notwithstanding its documented effectiveness across a range of learners and across various subject areas, DI is controversial and sometimes meets with criticism because of its emphasis on the 'teacher as activator', rather than 'teacher as facilitator'.

The strategy

DI has 12 main features:

1 *Explicit, systematic instruction.* Lessons are planned in the most logical, developmental order. They are highly structured and targeted skills are taught in a pre-planned manner.
2 *Scripted lesson plans.* Educators work through a carefully graduated sequence of tasks with carefully timed comments.
3 *Emphasis on pace.* In order to maximize students' engagement and prevent them from being distracted, DI lessons include many opportunities to respond.
4 *High level of success.* Although a brisk pace is maintained, the over-arching aim of every DI lesson is mastery. Lessons should be completed with 90% or better engagement and success rates.
5 *Frequent opportunities to practice targeted skills.* DI provides many opportunities for learners to practice and review material (see also **Strategy 60**). As well as supervised practice, independent practice is built in, e.g. through homework.
6 *Frequent curriculum-based assessment.* Short mastery tests are used periodically to ensure all learners have mastered the material (see also **Strategy 51**).
7 *Ability grouping.* Generally, learners are taught in small groups of 8 to12. They are grouped and re-grouped on the basis of their rate of progress. These temporary skill groups are not permanent tracks or streams (see also **Strategy 36**).
8 *Mediated scaffolding.* Gradually, the DI educator moves from an educator-guided to a more learner-guided approach.
9 *Embedded in other instructional strategies.* A school that uses DI does not use it all day. Rather, it would most likely be used at the beginning of some class periods and to review previous concepts.
10 *Strategic integration.* Instruction is integrated within and across subjects.
11 *Lesson closure.* Lessons have clear conclusions, with the educator summing up what the goals were and how they have been achieved.
12 *Practice.* Once the content or skill has been initially mastered, it is essential that the knowledge is rehearsed and the skill practised. This may take the form of guided or independent practice (see **Strategy 60**).

Source

What really works, Chapter 16. Op cit.

Strategy 65: Employ effective feedback

Rationale

How am I doing? This is a question many of us ask when we are learning a new skill or concept. We like to know if we are progressing in the right direction, with a view to improving our performance. In other words, we desire feedback, whether from a teacher, a parent, a friend, a computer or our own self-evaluation.

In classrooms, teachers should be communicating information to learners about their performance to enable them to modify their thinking or behaviour for the purpose of improving their learning.

Providing plenty of feedback does not necessarily mean using lots of tests or being overly prescriptive in giving directions to learners. Rather, it means providing information on how and why they understand or misunderstand, and how they can improve. Feedback is intended to be helpful, not embarrassing, and is part of the joint search for success.

Hattie's (2009) synthesis of feedback studies yielded a high effect size of 0.73, which he described as being among the most powerful influences on achievement.

The strategy

The purposes of feedback are to motivate learners, to inform them how well they have done and, above all, to show them how they can improve. To achieve these purposes, feedback should be:

- *timely*: provided as soon as possible after formative assessment has been conducted;
- *explicit:* indicates where the learner was accurate or inaccurate;
- *focused on strategy use, rather than on the learner's ability or effort* (i.e. 'You got it right because you applied the steps in the right order');
- *adjusted to the complexity of the task*: for low-level skills such as memorizing spelling words, immediate 'correct/incorrect' is more effective than delayed feedback. More complex tasks, such as drawing conclusions from two statements, lend themselves to more complex feedback, including reminding learners about relevant strategies;
- *provided in manageable units* to avoid cognitive overload; and
- *able to be used by learners*: they may need to be taught how to use feedback and to periodically check they are using previous feedback in their subsequent work.

In giving feedback, teachers should avoid making normative comparisons, giving overall grades, presenting feedback that discourages learners or threatens their self-esteem and interrupting them if they are actively engaged on a task.

Sources

Hattie, J. (2009). *Visible learning*. Routledge.
What really works, Chapter 17. Op cit.

Strategy 66: Employ assistive technology

Rationale

An assistive technology (AT) device is defined in US legislation as 'any item, piece of equipment, or product system, whether acquired commercially off the shelf, modified, or customized, that is used to increase, maintain, or improve functional capabilities of children with disabilities.'

The use of high-tech AT has only been with us since the 1980s, when the first major developments of computer-assisted instruction began to be used, but since then it has burgeoned. It enables individuals to have greater control over their own lives; contribute more fully to activities in their home, school and work environments; and interact to a greater extent with non-disabled individuals. Given the rapid advances in technology in general and AT in particular, it is an ever-expanding field, with enormous future possibilities.

The strategy

There are literally hundreds of AT devices, so I can only mention a few of them in this strategy. They range from low-tech (those that are not electronically based or battery-operated and usually low-cost, such as whiteboards and photo albums) to high-tech (those that are electronically-based and usually high-cost, such as computers, video cameras and voice output devices).

There are several groups of learners who would benefit from having access to AT. To take just three examples:

1   Those who have poor accuracy in locating the desired key, or are prone to accidentally pressing keys adjacent to the required one, or are unable to drag on the mouse. These could be helped by such adaptations as (a) expanded keyboards; (b) joysticks rather than a mouse, which can be moved directly with mouth, fingers, feet, elbows, etc. to control the cursor; (c) touch screens, where the user can touch objects directly on the screen and move them around; and (d) alternate input devices such as tracker systems that detect eye movements and speech.
2   Those who have limited control of their limbs or head and unable to use a standard keyboard and mouse. These could benefit from using a switch or a voice recognition programme as input devices.
3   Those who are partially sighted or blind and have difficulty in seeing the cursor and the information displayed on a screen. These may benefit from a larger monitor or having images of material from books maps etc. transmitted to a screen where they are enlarged, while blind learners could use screen readers to speak the text via speech synthesizers.

Source

What really works, Chapter 18. Op cit.

Strategy 67: Employ augmentative and alternative communication

Rationale

Some learners have significant difficulties in communicating with others using speech. These include those with cerebral palsy, autism, developmental apraxia, multiple sclerosis, stroke and traumatic brain injury, some of whom have virtually no speech ability, while others have some use of their voice.

There are two strategies for assisting these learners: *augmentative communication* and *alternative communication* (AAC). Augmentative communication is used to supplement whatever existing methods of communication a learner has. For example, a learner with delayed speech might use a touch screen computer or a voice output communication aid to communicate. Alternative communication represents an attempt to replace the lost means of communication. For example, learners who are born profoundly deaf can be taught sign language.

In most cases, speech and language therapists are most closely involved with AAC, but educators need to be knowledgeable about it if any learners in their classrooms are using it.

The strategy

The central goal of AAC is to provide learners with communication disorders with the opportunity and capability to: (a) interact in conversations, (b) participate more fully in activities at home, school and recreation, (c) learn their native language, and (d) establish and maintain their social roles.

Learners who use AAC usually employ many modalities (e.g. any existing speech or vocalizations, and gestures), in addition to various devices such as communication boards and speech-output communication aids. Most recently, these opportunities have expanded through smartphone technologies. As well, exponential advances are currently being made in the development of AAC apps on iPhones, iPods, iPads and Android devices. Voice Output Communication Aids (Speech Generating Devices), electronic devices that produce synthetic or digitized speech output, are increasingly in use. A variety of graphic symbols can be used in conjunction with VOCAs to represent messages activated when an individual uses a finger, hand or some other means to select a symbol from the VOCA's display.

The Picture Exchange Communication System (PECS) is perhaps the most widely used of all AAC systems. In PECS, learners are taught to pick up cards with line drawings or symbols on them and hand them to another person (educator, parent, peer, etc.), in exchange for the actual item. Once the learner can accomplish this simple request routine, the system is gradually expanded to teach such communication skills as labelling and information- seeking.

See also **Strategy 66**.

Source

What really works, Chapter 19. Op cit.

Strategy 68: Employ phonological awareness and processing

Rationale

Reading calls upon learners' ability to segment words into syllables and sounds, to identify where a specific sound occurs in a word and to blend sounds (phonemes) into words. These skills are referred to as *phonological awareness*. Weaknesses here account for a significant proportion of beginning reading problems. In order to prevent these from occurring, phonological awareness and processing strategies are necessary.

Phonological awareness calls upon the ability to notice, reflect upon and manipulate the individual sounds in words. In spoken English, this involves learning to discriminate between 43 phonemes (25 consonant phonemes and 18 vowel phonemes).

In turn, *phonemic awareness* is the recognition that sounds paired with letters are one and the same as the sounds of speech. Languages vary in the extent to which letters in print form (orthography) and sounds are associated. This is sometimes referred to as the degree of 'transparency'. For example, English has low transparency whereas Hungarian and Finnish have high transparency.

The strategy

The purpose of phonological awareness instruction is to develop oral language skills. This involves two processes: (a) the awareness that speech is made up of sounds, and (b) the ability to break down these sounds and manipulate them.

A useful framework is to divide activities into three groups:

> *Listening strategies.* The goal is to help learners to develop active, attentive and analytical listening skills. Here are some activities: (a) bring in recordings of various everyday sounds and ask learners to identify them, (b) ask them to listen to familiar poems and songs and occasionally replace certain words with nonsense words and ask them whether they noticed, and (c) with learners sitting in a circle, ask them to begin whispering certain words to the child next to them (sometimes referred to as 'Chinese Whispers').

> *Word-level strategies.* These activities aim at helping learners become aware that words can stand alone. They include: (a) have them count and distinguish syllables in a word, (b) have them add and delete syllables from a word, and (c) ask them to replace parts of a word with a different syllable.

> *Phonemic/rhyming strategies.* To facilitate learners' awareness of sound structures in words, teachers could: (a) ask them to find words that begin with particular sounds, (b) have them say what is left when a given sound or syllable is dropped from a word, and (c) have them select words that sound alike from a variety of pictures/words.

Source

What really works, Chapter 20. Op cit.

Strategy 69: Develop a positive and safe classroom climate

Rationale

Children learn better when they have positive perceptions of their classrooms' psychological environment. They learn better within an emotionally safe and predictable environment that is motivating and promotes positive goal-setting. Such environments help considerably to narrow the achievement gap between low- and high-SES learners.

The strategy

A positive classroom climate is characterized by three main features:

Positive relationships

Learners with special educational needs often experience emotions associated with failure, rejection and even experience hostility from others. Many have learned neither to trust their learning environment nor their own ability to survive in it. Educators should:

- understand learners' emotions and how they facilitate or hinder their motivation to learn.
- set up learning environments that emphasize positive emotions and reduce negative ones as far as possible; and
- provide environments characterized by stability, security, warmth, empathy, affirmation, support, a sense of community and justice and peace.

Personal development

Teachers should ensure children's classroom experiences facilitate their personal growth and self-enhancement. They should:

- *Help learners to set goals* Some learners with special educational needs may so devalue their abilities that they do not set goals; others may set goals far beyond their capacity; still others may set goals that are socially inappropriate. Teachers should: (a) help learners to set goals; (b) often talk about goals, show how lessons fit in with these, and help learners reflect on their progress towards these same goals; and (c) use direct, frequent, targeted feedback to maintain commitment to goals (see also **Strategy 65**).
- *Fully consider learners' cultural and language backgrounds.*
- *Provide a motivating learning environment.* Here are a couple of suggestions on motivation in general: (a) recognize that a learner's goals, emotions and personal agency beliefs are intrinsically valid to that person, and must be respected as the reality to be dealt with; and (b) be patient, but firm, with learners who have chronic low motivation.

System maintenance

Teachers should:

- Convey high, but realistic, expectations (see **Strategy 53**).
- Be authoritative, not authoritarian.

- Establish clear and essential rules.
- Take up appropriate positions in the classroom.

Note: many of these principles apply also to 'school climate' (see Berkowitz et al., 2016).

Sources

Berkowitz, R., Moore, H., Astor, R.A., Benbenbishty, R., & Astor, R.A. (2016). 'A research synthesis of the associations between socioeconomic background, inequality, school climate, and academic achievement.' *Review of Educational Research, 87*(2), 425–469.
What really works, Chapter 24. Op cit.

Strategy 70: Ensure that pedagogy is culturally sensitive

Rationale

Most western countries are becoming increasingly culturally diverse, a trend that poses a challenge to educators at all levels, but particularly in classrooms.

Students from different cultural groups come to school with a wide range of experiences associated with their ethnicities. Some will be members of minorities with long histories in the country, perhaps with histories of discrimination or persecution arising from colonization or even slavery. Still others will be immigrants or refugees who may suffer from trauma associated with conflict in their country of origin, or have been exposed to religious persecution. Many new arrivals will not speak the language of their host country.

The strategy

Several approaches are called for:

- *Emphasize positive relationships with students.* The quality of the in-class face-to-face relationships and interactions between students and their teachers is critical.
- *Set uniform standards across all ethnic groups.* A major impediment to many (but not all) ethnic groups' educational achievement is teachers' low expectations, which create self-fulfilling prophesies of school failure.
- *Support students' linguistic acquisition and development.* Teachers should support their students' language of schooling and languages they use outside the school. Teachers should also be aware of the linguistic demands of the curriculum and seek to make it accessible to students from a variety of language backgrounds and at different stages of competence in the language of schooling (see also **Strategies 11** and **12**).
- *Engage with families of all students, including those from ethnic minorities.* Parents and caregivers play a major role in the development and education of their children. The challenge for educators is to create collaborative relationships by recognizing parents/ family members as valuable partners in promoting academic progress and,by working with them from a posture of cultural reciprocity, mutual respect, open communication, shared responsibility and collaboration (see also **Strategy 80**).
- *Take account of different worldviews of students and their families.* See **Strategy 49**.
- *Ensure that curricula content reflects consideration of cultural diversity.* The content of what is taught in schools should be carefully selected and presented to take account of the cultural diversity of students. One of the aims should be to eliminate prejudices about culturally distinct groups. Older students should be helped to understand, investigate and determine how implicit cultural assumptions, frames of references and biases within disciplines influence the ways in which knowledge is constructed.

Source

Diversities in education, Chapter 4. Op cit.

Strategy 71: Educate students to be citizens of diverse societies in a globalized world

Rationale

Today, we face many interconnected global challenges, including nuclearization, climate change, migration and conflict. Global citizenship education (GCE) is one means to help young people develop the knowledge, skills, behaviours, attitudes and values to engage in effective action at their local levels, with an eye towards a more just and peaceful future at the global level (Anderson & Bhattacharya, 2017).

GCE is a form of learning that involves students' active participation in projects that address global issues of a social, political, economic or environmental nature. It is underpinned by principles of human rights, social justice and inclusiveness.

The UK Oxfam Curriculum for Global Citizenship (1997, p. 1) defines a global citizen as someone who:

- is aware of the wider world and has a sense of their own role as a world citizen;
- respects and values diversity;
- has an understanding of how the world works economically, politically, socially, culturally, technologically and environmentally;
- is outraged by social injustice;
- is willing to act to make the world a more equitable and sustainable place; and
- participates in and contributes to the community at a range of levels.

GCE is one of the strategic areas of UNESCO's programme for the period 2014–2021. Its work in this field is guided by the Sustainable Development Goals of *Education 2030: Agenda and Framework for Action*.

The strategy

UNESCO provides the following framework for GCE objectives (examples only):

1   *Local, national, and global systems and structures,*

- Describe how the local environment is organized and how it relates to the wider world, and introduce the concept of citizenship.
- Identify governance structures, decision-making processes and dimensions of citizenship.
- Discuss how global governance structures interact with national and local structures and explore global citizenship.

2   *Issues affecting interaction and connectedness of communities at local, national and global levels.*

- List key local, national and global issues and explore how these may be connected.
- Investigate the reasons behind major common global concerns and their impact at national and local levels.

3   *Underlying assumptions and power dynamics.*

- Name different sources of information and develop basic skills for inquiry.
- Differentiate between fact/opinion, reality/fiction, and different viewpoints/perspectives.
- Investigate underlying assumptions and describe inequalities and power dynamics.

Sources

Anderson, K., & Bhattacharya, J. (2017). *Measuring global citizenship education: A collection of practices and tools.* Brookings.

Diversities in education, Chapter 4. Op cit.

Oxfam (1997). *A curriculum for global citizenship.* Oxford.

7

FAMILIES

What counts?

In many western societies, the notion of what constitutes a family is undergoing rapid and profound changes. Until recently, definitions focused on the *nuclear family*. This typically comprised a married (usually) couple – a mother and father – and their child(ren). Earlier, in addition to the nuclear family, grandparents and other relatives were frequently part of the mix, making up the *extended family*.

Nowadays, there is an almost bewildering array of family types. In addition to nuclear and extended families, we have:

- unmarried heterosexual couples raising children;
- gay, lesbian or transgender couples raising children;
- single women having children without a partner to help raise them;
- single men having children without a partner to help raise them;
- a re-constituted (or blended) family – two partners living in one household with one or more children from one or both partners' previous relationships and/or from the current relationship; and
- a heterosexual, gay, lesbian or transgender couple living together without children.

Because of this diversity (and there may be other family types), it may be appropriate to use a broader definition of the family, such as 'a group of people who are related by either blood or marriage/similar form of committed relationship' (see www.encyclopedia.com/social-sciences/dictionaries-thesauruses-pictures-and-press-releases/family-sociology).

In recent decades, there have been marked shifts in the composition of families in western countries. For example, in the United States, in 1960, 87% of families had two parents, while this had dropped to 69% by 2014. Correspondingly, the relevant figures for one-parent households had increased from 9% to 26% (www.pewsocialtrends.org/2015/12/17/1-the-american-family-today/).

There is also evidence that people of different ethnicities are more likely to live in certain types of households. Thus, in the United States, the proportion of two-parent households in 2014 among Whites was 78%, compared with 67% among Hispanics and only 38% among Blacks. Similar ethnic differences have been noted in New Zealand's single-parent households: European (8%,) Asian (10%), Pacific Island (14%) and Maori(19%) (https://teara.govt.nz/mi/graph/31594/household-types-by-ethnicity-2004). In the United Kingdom, an even higher proportion of single-parenthood was noted among African-Caribbean households, 48% of which were headed by lone parents (women) (https://sociologytwynham.com/2008/07/08/family-diversity-ethnicity/).

The main message to take from this diversity is that educators must not assume that the nuclear family with two parents is the only type of family.

Strategy 72: Develop parent training programmes

Rationale

There is widespread agreement that many children from low-SES backgrounds are brought up in less than optimal environments, with less than half of them being ready for school when first enrolled. In the first few years of life many of these children are exposed to considerably fewer words and a limited linguistic code as compared with peers from high-SES homes. Other factors include: differential access to books and the Internet, and parents' lack of knowledge of how to make their way around the education system. Parent training programmes are aimed at helping parents/caregivers acquire effective parenting skills.

The strategy

While parent training programmes are normally designed and delivered by specialists such as psychologists, it is important for teachers to be aware of what these involve. As well, they may work in collaboration with parents and professionals involved in any training programme. For example, they may describe child behaviours of concern, as well as any positive behaviours. In addition, it is important that classroom strategies are consistent with those that parents may be using at home.

Two programmes serve to illustrate what is involved:

> *Parent Management Training.* This programme helps parents use effective behavioural management strategies with their children. It is based on the assumption that children's conduct problems result from maladaptive parent–child interactions, such as paying attention to deviant behaviour, ineffective use of commands and harsh punishments. Thus, parents are trained to define and monitor their child's behaviour, avoid coercive interchanges and positively reinforce acceptable behaviour by implementing developmentally appropriate consequences for their child's defiance. Such parent training includes a mixture of didactic instruction, live or videotaped modelling and role-plays. The emphasis is on teaching behavioural strategies (see also **Strategy 62**).

> *Incredible Years Programme.* This is aimed at children aged from birth to 12 years and their parents. It comprises a series of two-hours per week group discussions. The programme contains videotaped modeling sessions, which show a selection from 250 vignettes of approximately 2 minutes each in which parents interact with their children in both appropriate and inappropriate ways. After each vignette, the therapist leads a discussion of the relevant interactions and solicits parents' responses. Parents are taught play and reinforcement skills, effective limit-setting and nonviolent discipline techniques, problem-solving approaches promoting learning and development, and ways to become involved in their children's schooling.

Sources

Diversities in education, Chapter 6. Op cit.
What really works, Chapter 7. Op cit.

Strategy 73: Engage families in education

Rationale

Parents and caregivers play a major role in the development and education of their children. The OECD considers linking schools with parents and communities to be one of its top five recommendations for addressing the needs of low-SES students. It points out that disadvantaged parents tend to be less involved in their children's schooling, for multiple economic and social reasons. In contrast, engaged parents encourage more positive attitudes towards school, improve homework habits, reduce absenteeism, disengagement and dropout, and enhance academic achievement.

There are many good reasons why educators should seek to develop effective relationships with the parents of the children they teach. Several stand out:

- Parents are most probably the only people involved with their child's education throughout their entire school years.
- Parents know their child's development better than anyone else.
- Parents can help educators to gain a better understanding of some aspects of their child's behaviour.
- Working with parents increases the likelihood of consistency in expectations of behaviour at home and at school.
- By being closely involved, parents will gain a better understanding of their children's schooling and the school's vision and goals.
- Children will receive positive messages about the importance of their education if they see their parents and their teachers working together.
- In many countries, it is a legal requirement for professionals to consult with parents of children with special educational needs in the development of Individual Education Plans.

The strategy

The challenge for educators is to create collaborative relationships with parents/caregivers by recognizing them as valuable partners in promoting academic progress. This requires working with them from a posture of cultural reciprocity, mutual respect, open communication, shared responsibility and collaboration.

There are five different levels of parent involvement:

Level 1: Being informed: the school informs parents about its programmes and, in turn, is asked for information.

Level 2: Taking part in activities: parents are involved in activities, but to a limited extent.

Level 3: Dialogue and exchange of views: parents are invited to examine school or classroom goals and needs.

Level 4: Taking part in decision making: parents are asked for their views when decisions affecting their child are being made.

Level 5: Having responsibility to act: parents make decisions in partnership with the school and are involved in both planning and evaluating parts of the school programme.

Sources

Diversities in education, Chapters 3 and 4. Op cit.
What really works, Chapter 7. Op cit.

8

THE CHILD

Constructor of knowledge

As we come to the final aspect of my ecological model – the child – I should like to correct any impression I may have given that education is something adults *do* to children. Rather, I believe that children themselves significantly contribute to their own learning processes. They learn from their experiences, select what they attend to and work out their own 'rules of the game'. Increasingly, with the ubiquitous Internet, children are independently choosing what, how and from whom to learn. They are active participants in their own development and not mere clay being shaped by forces around them.

From the moment of birth, human beings actively process the world about them and find patterns and meaning in their experiences. Thus, they come to learn the language of their cultures and the appropriate social rules and roles. They learn to walk, to run and to engage in complex interactions and games with their family and friends. They learn to be creative, to make new things and to work out new ways of solving problems. In short, human beings are natural learners. While parents, siblings, friends and teachers mediate some of this learning, much of it is independent and self-regulated. Much of it is spontaneous and occurs through observation and trial and error.

However, I recognize that, notwithstanding this common drive to learn, there is considerable variation among individuals in what and how they learn. Some of this diversity reflects variations in biological structures and functions, while some reflects variations in cultural experiences and factors such as exposure to the trauma of war, conflict, natural disasters, inadequate diet, abuse and poor living conditions.

It is our task as adults to enhance children's natural proclivity for learning. This means we should respect children as active constructors of knowledge and, by-and- large, as being capable of driving their own learning. We should adopt a child-centred, whole-child approach in teaching that recognizes the importance of achieving creativity and emotional goals, as well as cognitive goals. Above all, our task is to help learners achieve the best possible quality of life.

Source

What Really Works, Preface. Op cit.

Strategy 74: Build on students' play interests

Rationale

Picking up the theme of children being active constructors of their own knowledge, I turn now to exploring how play can contribute to this process. From the outset, let me say that the value of play in children's development goes beyond the preschool age. Rather, it also has an important role in children's learning in primary and secondary schools; indeed, it is a lifelong process. Play greatly contributes to cognitive and language development, emotional well-being, relationship formation and self-regulation.

According to Whitebread et al. (2012), there are five main types of play in which children engage:

1   *physical play*: active exercise (e.g. jumping, climbing), rough-and-tumble (with friends, siblings or parents) and fine-motor practice (e.g. sewing, colouring);
2   *play with objects*: building, making and constructing;
3   *symbolic play*: spoken language, reading and writing, number, various visual media (painting, drawing, collage), music;
4   *pretend/socio-dramatic play*: following the social rules governing the characters they are portraying; and
5   *games with rules*: physical games such as chasing, hide-and-seek, throwing and catching, board and card games, electronic and computer games, and sporting activities.

Opportunities to play are not always available to some children. Some, particularly in crowded urban areas, may have limited access to natural and outdoor play opportunities. Some have their waking hours filled with schoolwork and extra after-school classes. Some have minimal access to play materials, often through poverty. Some may be restricted by risk-averse parents who perceive their environments to be dangerous. Still others may have play opportunities restricted by teachers who consider learning a more serious activity that should focus instead on reading, writing, listening and speaking within the four walls of a classroom. Adults vary, too, in the extent to which they participate in children's play. Children's play activities are also subject to various cultural and religious strictures, particularly concerning girls' activities. These and other factors probably account for the sharp decline in children's free play with other children in western countries (Chudakoff, 2007).

The strategy

Teachers should examine their programmes to ensure children are provided with opportunities to exercise all five types of play in their daily activities. In their communication with parents/caregivers, they should point out the value of play, especially engagement with their children in play activities.

Sources

Chudakoff, H.P. (2007). *Children at play: An American history*. New York University Press.
Whitebread, D., Basilio, M., Kuvalja, M., & Verma, M. (2012). *The importance of play*. University of Cambridge.

Strategy 75: Develop personalized learning

Rationale

For the most part in this book, I have emphasized the importance of looking at diversity in terms of individual differences rather than exclusively in terms of group membership. The best way forward is individualization or, as some put it, 'personalization'. This involves varying content, activities, teaching, learning, methods and resources to take into account the range of interests, needs and experiences of individual students. With advances in technology, it is increasingly feasible to put this approach into operation.

Underlying personalization is the principle of differentiation. Perhaps the best known advocate of differentiation is Carol Ann Tomlinson (2014), who asserted that teachers should differentiate three aspects of the curriculum:

> *Content*: refers to the concepts, principles and skills that teachers want students to learn. All students should be given access to the same core content, teachers addressing the same concepts with all students but adjusting the degree of complexity.

> *Process*: refers to the activities that help students make sense of the ideas and skills being taught. Teachers can modify these activities to provide some students with more complexity and others with more scaffolding, depending on their readiness levels.

> *Products*: different students can create different products, based on their readiness levels, interests and learning preferences.

The strategy

Personalized learning has the following features (Institute for Personalized Learning; Rickbaugh, 2016):

- it is designed around an individual learner's readiness, strengths, needs and interests;
- learners are active participants in setting goals, planning learning paths, tracking progress and determining how they will demonstrate what they have learned;
- at any given time, learning objectives, content, methods and pacing are likely to vary from learner to learner;
- the teacher plays an active role in setting individual learning goals aligned to standards, planning what and how students will learn, identifying the resources they will need, and determining how they should demonstrate their learning; and
- it requires a leveraging of modern technologies, which help to track and manage the learning needs of all students and provide a platform to access myriad content, resources and learning opportunities needed to meet each student's needs everywhere at any time.

Sources

Diversities in education, Chapter 6. Op cit.
Institute for Personalized Learning. URL: http://institute4pl.org/
Rickbaugh, J. (2016). *Tapping the power of personalized learning*. Alexandria, VA: ASCD.
Tomlinson, C.A. (2014). *The differentiated classroom: Responding to the needs of learners*. Second edition. Alexandria, VA: ASCD.

Strategy 76: Develop self-regulated learning

Rationale

In free, democratic societies, people expect and are expected to exercise autonomy by setting goals, making choices and taking decisions over most aspects of their lives. One of the features of maturity and a good quality of life in most societies is the ability to take responsibility for one's own actions.

Thus, a major objective of education should be to assist all learners to be increasingly involved in making decisions about their own learning and to act on these decisions.

Although self-determination (or self-control) is a valued attribute, it is frequently the case that many learners with special educational needs seem to have little control over their lives, depending instead on those around them to make decisions on their behalf. This need not remain the case for there is growing evidence that such children, including those with major disabilities, can be helped to take more control over their own learning.

There is substantial evidence for the effectiveness of teaching self-regulating skills. A recent study, for example, concluded that: (a) there is a positive overall relationship between self-regulation and academic achievement; (b) individual elements of self-regulation (e.g. attitudes towards learning, attention and persistence) are also related to academic achievement; and (c) aspects of self-regulation such as attention, persistence, flexibility, motivation and confidence can all be improved as a result of effective teaching (Duckworth et al., 2009).

The strategy

Here are some guidelines for developing self-regulated learning skills in learners:

- foster self-control through a long-term positive relationship with a dependable person who communicates its value;
- set self-control challenges within the skill range of individual learners;
- expose learners to a wide range of positive models of the successful exercise of self-control, e.g. in sports;
- engage them in simulations involving self-control challenges;
- motivate them to exert effort and persist in the face of difficulty;
- help them to define short and long-term goals and set priorities among them;
- teach decision-making skills when deciding what actions to take that would increase the likelihood of achieving the goals; and
- teach self-monitoring skills, e.g. by observing one's own target behaviours and recording them.

See also **Strategy 57**.

Sources

Duckworth, K., Akerman, R., MacGregor, A., Salter, E., & Vorhaus, J. (2009). *Self- regulated learning: A literature review. Research Report 33*. London: Centre for Research on the Wider Benefits of Learning, Institute of Education, University of London.
What really works, Chapter 9. Op cit.

9

CONCLUSIONS

It is time to radically re-think our education systems

My purpose in writing this book was to stimulate discussion on how education systems around the world could – indeed, should – improve the quality of education they provide for their most vulnerable children. In the main, these comprise children from some ethnic minorities, those from low-SES homes, children with disabilities, and, in some countries, girls and those with certain religious beliefs. Given the increasing diversity in many countries, this is an urgent matter to attend to.

Educators have a responsibility to maximize opportunities for all children to learn and, as a corollary, remove barriers to learning. I hope that the 78 strategies I have presented in this book will contribute to this endeavour. As well as our moral and legal obligations to provide a sound education for disadvantaged children, there are also social and economic benefits to society. In other words, there is interest convergence.

To help disadvantaged children fulfill their potential, whole systems of education need to be re-designed. We simply cannot carry on with policies and practices that have failed and continue to fail so many of these children. After all, as Einstein is attributed as having said, insanity is doing the same thing over and over again and expecting different results.

In advancing my ecological model, I have noted that everything is connected to everything else. This means that change must be coordinated at all levels of our education systems – from government, through bureaucracies, communities, schools, classrooms and families. It will require all of us, whatever our role in education, to 'speak truth to power', as the Quakers once said.

I have also emphasized that educational policies and practices should draw upon abundant research-based evidence and international best practice. The challenge is to bring well-founded strategies to scale and put aside strategies that have self-evidently failed. Here I am reminded of a story from the Book of Buddha. It concerns a man who goes on a journey and comes to a river. It is very wide and very deep, but he is determined to cross it. He looks around a sees several logs, which he manages to tie together to form a raft. He paddles it across the river. Then, when he reaches the other side, he puts the raft on his back and he carries it around wherever he goes: across the desert, up mountains… He is so grateful that the raft was able to help him in his moment of need, he can't put it aside, even when it has ceased to serve a purpose. We must put such rafts aside once they have outlived their purpose, and especially so when they have never served a useful purpose at all.

I conclude with two high-priority, over-arching strategies.

Strategy 77: Recruit, train and retain high quality teachers

Rationale

There can be little doubt that teachers, school leaders and teacher educators play a critical role in improving the outcomes of students who are, for one or more reasons, disadvantaged. The challenges require educators who are sensitive to and welcoming of diversity among their students, who are willing and able to understand and accept different world views, who are able to develop and implement curricula based on the principles of universal design for learning, who are able to adapt their pedagogy to take account of the diverse needs of their students, and who are prepared to employ evidence-informed policies and practices. This means that teachers and school leaders must be educated to discharge these responsibilities, both in their initial teacher education programmes and later in their ongoing professional development. In turn, this draws attention to the important role played by teacher educators and their accountability in preparing teachers to work with diverse learners.

The strategy

Five areas need to be emphasized:

1   Initial teacher education programmes should contain significant reference to diverse learners. This should permeate all components of such programmes and not be limited to a dedicated course.
2   In-service professional development programmes for educators should offer on-going courses on student diversity. Such courses should be offered through 'communities of learning' in which all educators in a particular site or cluster of schools in a particular community participate in shared learning.
3   Attention should be paid to up-skilling teacher educators in current developments in educating diverse learners.
4   Research into educating diverse learners should be actively encouraged, with an emphasis on extending the evidence base for teaching such learners.
5   Every effort should be made to ensure that high-quality teachers are employed in schools with a high proportion of diverse learners. This may require providing appropriate incentives, and certainly ensuring that high-quality ongoing professional development is made available. As well, mentoring and supervision programmes for novice teachers should be put in place.

Source

Diversities in education, Chapters 3, 4, 6 and 7. Op cit.

Strategy 78: Provide innovative and effective leadership at all levels

Rationale

In this book I have traversed 78 strategies to meet the challenge in educating diverse learners. Responsibility for implementing them falls to a wide range of people: politicians, national education departments or ministries, provincial or state departments bureaucrats, community leaders, school principals, teachers, and so on. For change to occur, leadership must be exercised at all these levels. Moreover, there should be agreement that there is indeed a crisis to be addressed and that there needs to be a coordinated approach to solving it. Obviously, I recommend that the agenda that should be followed by personnel at the various levels of the system are the strategies I have summarized in this book.

The strategy

Here are some of the important leadership roles that need to be exercised throughout an education system in order to bring about change:

- *providing and selling a vision*: defining the problem and articulating the vision of a way forward;
- *providing encouragement and recognition*: identifying and recognizing those who are promoting and implementing innovative ways of addressing the problem;
- *obtaining resources*: advocating for adequate resources to be made available and equitably distributed to implement change; and
- *monitoring improvement*: increasingly, it is not acceptable for leaders just to 'do good', but to show that their policies and practices are having a positive impact on learners.

More specifically, evidence suggests that the total (direct and indirect) effects of *school leadership* on student achievement account for about one-quarter of total school effects, and probably more in disadvantaged schools. A recent OECD (2012) report identified school leadership as one of five priority recommendations in supporting improvements in low performing disadvantaged schools. Specifically, it advocated:

- developing school leadership preparation programmes;
- reinforcing coaching and mentoring programmes for school leaders;
- developing strategies to attract and retain competent leaders in low performing disadvantaged schools; and
- providing systemic support for re-structuring and re-culturing schools whenever necessary.

Leadership should also be exercised by researchers and professional bodies with an interest in education. This can best be provided by the generation and dissemination of research findings, the critical analyses of policies and advocacy of social justice and equity.

Sources

Diversities in education, Chapter 3. Op cit.
OECD (2012). *Equity and quality in education: Supporting disadvantaged students and schools*. Paris.
What really works, Chapters 25 and 27. Op cit.

INDEX

Note: For multiple-authored sources, only the first-named author is included.

Printed in Great Britain
by Amazon

10870472R00066